HENRY KNIGHT MILLER

# Henry Fielding's *Tom Jones* and the Romance Tradition

English Literary Studies
University of Victoria

1976

© 1976 by Henry Knight Miller

ELS Editions
Department of English
University of Victoria
Victoria, BC
Canada V8W 3W1
*www.elseditions.com*

Founding Editor: Samuel L. Macey

General Editor: Luke Carson

Printed by CreateSpace

No part of this publication may be reproduced, stored in a retrieval system or transmitted, in any form or by any means. Without the prior written consent of the publisher or a licence from The Canadian Copyright Licensing Agency (Access Copyright). For an Access Copyright licence, visit *www.accesscopyright.ca* or call toll free to 1–800–893–5777.

English literary studies monograph series
ISSN 0829-7681 ; 6
ISBN-10 1-530029-12-0
ISBN-13 978-1-530029-12-9

# CONTENTS

| | | |
|---|---|---|
| Preface | | 5 |
| CHAPTER 1 | Introduction | 7 |
| CHAPTER 2 | *Mythos* / Questions of Plot and Structure | 22 |
| CHAPTER 3 | *Time and Place* / Questions of Setting | 42 |
| CHAPTER 4 | *People* / The Characters | 56 |
| CHAPTER 5 | *Ethos* / The Dimension of Meaning | 72 |
| CHAPTER 6 | *Logos* / Questions of Style | 85 |
| Notes | | 102 |

# PREFACE

An argument that presumes to question the unquestioned and to wander some distance from the steady paths of received truth and sanctioned vocabulary in modern criticism cannot reasonably hope to be popular; but it may well find shelter in a scholarly monograph. I welcome this opportunity to contribute to the Victoria ELS Monograph Series, not only for the excellent company it affords but also because the informed audience that may be expected for its papers will not search here for something that I have not sought to provide. What is offered is neither an introduction to *Tom Jones* nor an attempt to relate it to "The Novel" nor even a presumptuous effort to further its contemporary "popularity": my argument declares, rather, that *Tom Jones* is a comic Romance, a comic Epic in prose, unique and incomparable, and that it is thoroughly in the epic-romance tradition. Its affinities are with Ariosto and Cervantes, *Amadis de Gaule* and Sidney's *Arcadia*, and this means that it is not answerable to (and indeed will not fully answer to) modes of criticism proper enough to another literary realm but quite inadequate for the romance. Of course, art that has something of genuine importance to give will always transcend its own particular era and genre, as *Tom Jones* most assuredly has. But, as a moment's reflection on the world's masterpieces should convince us, great art must also seem always somewhat foreign to, distanced from, any later era's nearest and most immediate practical concerns. In this truth, indeed, lies the ultimate commentary upon "realism" in art, since "realism," by definition, must inevitably emphasize that which seems immediately and practically plausible for the local world of "today"—which is already departing.

My argument, therefore, like that of the larger work in progress from which this little study falls, is not at all a defense of the "realism" of Fielding or any other master of narrative art. My interest here is to exhibit as well as I can the total integration of the formal and semantic aspects of Henry Fielding's great fictive universe, something with which "realism," in today's sense, has very little to do. But the appropriate tradition and context for his work has much indeed to do with an adequate recognition of Fielding's artistic achievement, and that is my present concern. I may hope that my examination of *Tom Jones* in its appropriate tradition will offer some fresh perspectives not only upon that work but also perhaps upon the generic definition of Romance itself.

Again, although I am quite conscious of the sound and illuminating analyses that have over the years emphasized the contribution to Fielding's ultimate fictive mastery made by such literary modes as the drama and satire and the discursive essay, and such non-fictive narrative modes as history and biography, these (except for dramatic comedy, which is a central concern) are not to my present purpose. The fact that such studies are not cited does not mean, however, that I do not consider them of remarkable importance to our total picture of a most comprehensive artist. Considerations of space, which forbid a Bibliography, have made it impossible as well to record adequately in the footnotes all the many and various indebtednesses I have incurred. But the warmth of my appreciation is no less certain, for all that.

Citations from *Tom Jones* follow the definitive edition of Martin C. Battestin (Oxford, 1975), in The Wesleyan Fielding; but to avoid the awkward length of double references, I have given only the book and chapter numbers of the original.

HENRY KNIGHT MILLER

CHAPTER 1

# Introduction

"For the world of man is not only a world of things; it is a world of symbols where the distinction between reality and make-believe is itself unreal."—E. H. Gombrich, *Art and Illusion*

"I hope here be truths."—*Measure for Measure*

The long history of narrative fiction, like the history of dramatic literature, exhibits a more or less continuous line of writings, with certain notable lacunae and certain distinguishable nodes that can be (or have been) chronologically and geographically differentiated as Greek fiction or Greek drama, medieval fiction or medieval drama, and so on. Although such labels are more a matter of convenience than a key to any particular *Zeitgeist*, they have the very real and practical function of preparing the reader for a special and identifiable kind of literary experience.

Such is the case with the useful if not clear-cut distinction between the "Romance" and the "Novel." This distinction arose, of course, in somewhat confused circumstances that helped to spawn further confusions. Its origins, as can readily be seen in the preface to Congreve's *Incognita*, lie in the seventeenth-century conception of the *novella*; and in the eighteenth century the familiar convention gradually crystallized of separating out prose tales that dealt with contemporary or ordinary life and intrigues as "novels," and of reserving the previously most popular generic term for long fiction, "romance," to describe the prose (or verse) narratives that dealt with unordinary or aristocratic, and historically or geographically distant, "far-off" life. For a new middle-class audience Romance thus came to be associated with, on the one hand, chronologically "primitive" historical or pseudo-historical tales, and, on the other hand, with sheer fantasy and extravagance, or even—as an "escape" from actual bourgeois life—with high "idealism."[1] Hence the very misleading overtones (for later generations) of the adjective "Romantick," about which I shall have a later word.

From the early Renaissance through the Augustan period, however, the term "romance," though perhaps no more precise in delineation, had comprehended a body of narrative fiction that was not at all habitually thought of as remote from central human concerns—with an exception that I shall mention. The term was vaguely inclusive of such works as the Greek romances and Latin comic romances, the medieval romances both in verse and prose, the peninsular romances of Spain and Portugal, the *romanzi* (romance-epics or epic-romances) of Boiardo, Ariosto, Tasso, and the English Spenser and Milton, and the romances of Greene and Lyly and Sidney. The semantic decline in the authority of the word "romance" (although, of course, there had always been detractors) occurs historically as it comes to be increasingly referred to one particular kind of romance and its special audience—namely, the seventeenth-century *roman héroïque* and its ardent female readers. With respect to the earlier romance tradition, however, there were many critics from the Renaissance on to argue that there was no essential distinction between the romance and the epic, and that therefore the romancers who followed Homer and Virgil and Statius belonged altogether to the same high narrative tradition—a rational postulate supported by a distinguished modern classicist, who has flatly declared: "Romance and epic are basically the same genre, as much so as ancient and modern drama."[2]

Henry Fielding may very well have been seeking, legitimately enough, to identify his own prose romances with the dignity of the highest poetic kind by calling them Comic *Epics* in Prose; but, in following Cervantes (or at least the Canon of Toledo) who, along with the best critics of the Renaissance, had declared that the epic could be written in prose,[3] he was primarily acknowledging that this was the most important *narrative* model that was at once familiar to his audience and of unquestioned major stature as literature, as he could not escape knowing his own work was. Fielding employs the term "Epic" in the preface to *Joseph Andrews* both in the sense of a particular "Species of Poetry" and in the general sense of any narrative mode that has achieved literary distinction (including the romance); and he uses the specific word "Romance" for an extended fictional narrative in prose, i.e., a prose epic, or (negatively) for a mode that he considered sub-literary, such as the popular French "heroic romances" and their vulgarized offspring. Hence a "romance" of literary magnitude would be prose-epic, whereas the great works of Homer and Virgil (or the *romanzi* of Ariosto and Tasso) would be verse-epics. The serious verse-epic, such as the *Aeneid*, was complemented by the comic verse-epic, such as the lost "Homeric" *Margites* mentioned by Aristotle; and the "serious" prose-epic, such as Fénelon's influential *Télémaque*, was complemented by the comic prose-epic, such as *Don Quixote* or *Joseph Andrews*.[4] It is odd, and perhaps unfortunate, that Fielding's argument, so alive to the intelligent Renaissance distinctions, did not (instead of dragging in the *Margites*) exploit the separation often made by Renaissance critics and those of his own time between the *Iliad* as "tragic epic" (i.e., siege-epic or battle-epic) and the *Odyssey* as "comic epic" (i.e., quest-epic). For, like the bulk of the romances over the whole tradition, his own comic romances are quest-epics, and his only glance at the siege-epics occurs in the merely allusive mock-heroic rendering of their characteristic battle scenes.

The Renaissance view of narrative does, at any rate, focus upon those elements that epic and romance have in common; and since it is the perspective that was accepted by Henry Fielding, it is naturally the perspective that I shall assume, ignoring as quite irrelevant later Romantic and impressionistic notions (such as those of W. P. Ker and E. M. W. Tillyard) of what constitutes an "epic"—or, for that matter, a "romance." Every fiction has its "Let us suppose ... ," its own "coded" text that we must, as readers, individually decipher through whatever keys we possess; and it should be patent that the more nearly we allow ourselves to enter into any given fictive world on its own terms (the original encoding), the more comprehensive and valid our response and our understanding are likely to be. An able student of Renaissance fiction has observed that the romance tradition properly approached "will thus, instead of rendering for us the probabilities of life as we know it, attempt to enlarge our sense of the possibilities of life."[5]

Since my purpose is to argue that Fielding's *Tom Jones* is in all major essentials a "romance" and vitally profits from earlier modes of fiction, indeed, cannot be adequately interpreted—or "decoded"—unless the conventions of romance are imaginatively comprehended, what I should hope to do is briefly to display some of the central narrative conventions, structures, and motifs that would have constituted for Fielding a "usable past" in the romance tradition. Such a remembrance may help to provide terms for an appropriately literate "set" on the part of the sympathetic reader; for, clearly enough, the critical posture of what has been called by Messrs. Scholes and Kellogg our "almost hopelessly novel-centered" view of narrative literature[6] is one that can offer only dwarfish returns for a romance. The first qualification, C. S. Lewis has said, "for judging any piece of workmanship from a corkscrew to a cathedral is to know *what* it is—what it was intended to do and how it is meant to be used."[7] *Quid sit?* then is logically prior to *Quale sit?* and I shall argue that, despite his hostility to the French *roman héroïque*, Fielding did indeed think of his great work as a romance and that, like the *bricoleur* of Lévi-Strauss, he used the means at hand, drawing upon the vast composite "pool" of narrative possibilities, the rich fund of motifs, characters, episodes, themes, and structural forms that the Romance tradition—epic, prose fiction, and verse narrative—offered. This would have been the most obvious narrative tradition accessible in the eighteenth century to one who wished to think of prose fiction as a form of art.

There are two apparent qualifications that are not really qualifications to this statement (since they do not enter as high artistic traditions). One lies in the fact that the short prose-tale, the *novella*, tended in the seventeenth century to become the central native form of popular narrative in England,

and even romances were condensed for a popular audience, as one may see in Emanuel Forde's breathless *Ornatus and Artesia* (at the end of the sixteenth century, but often reprinted). The *novella* was, of course, the original "novel," and its short-form conventions would lie behind many of the interesting experiments in prose fiction in the eighteenth century.

The other significant phenomenon, as I have already suggested, is the so-called "heroic romance" of seventeenth-century France, unquestionably the most widely-read mode of long prose fiction in England in the seventeenth and early eighteenth centuries—and one which Henry Fielding instinctively saw as a trivializing and effeminizing of the entire tradition. The animus against "mere romances," which appears frequently in his discourse, can almost entirely be referred to "those voluminous Works commonly called Romances, namely *Clelia, Cleopatra, Astraea, Cassandra,* the *Grand Cyrus,* and innumerable others which contain, as I apprehend, very little Instruction or Entertainment."[8] As his allusion to "Monsieur Romance" in *Tom Jones* (13.1) would indicate, the negative sense of the term was automatically associated for him with the French productions that had corrupted the tradition; and he would significantly declare (9.1) that it was the contempt into which the art of fiction had been brought by such performances "that hath made us so cautiously avoid the Term Romance, a Name with which we might otherwise have been well enough contented."

The "heroic romance" arose in France as, in part, an offshoot of the extravagant sixteenth-century Spanish and French continuations of the great peninsular romance, *Amadís de Gaula*. But, from the famed *Astrée* of Honoré D'Urfé, a pastoral romance of the early seventeenth century that set the tone for what followed, the essential feature of the "heroic romance," unlike any earlier romances of the tradition (even those of the much misunderstood Chrétien de Troyes), was that it specifically aimed at and flattered the concerns of a female coterie. The inspiration for and frequently the lightly masked subject matter of the *roman à longue haleine* (which could run effortlessly to twelve volumes) was the *précieuse* salon, such as that of the renowned Hôtel de Rambouillet; and the most descriptive term for it would actually be "salon romance" rather than "heroic romance." For, despite a plethora of battle scenes and the incidental trappings of chivalric romance (substituting a puffed-up *gloire* for the *sapientia et fortitudo* of the earlier romance hero), the new stress in the typical salon romance was really upon feminine social and "psychological" concerns, the minute punctilios of "moral" conduct and social propriety, the internal state of the heart, and the casuistry of love—usually platonic love, for here, as almost never before in the long tradition of the romance (despite later clichés), the impeccably chaste heroine maintained an awful distance from her adoring servant. It is as though they took seriously what Cervantes had postulated comically (for he knew very well that the chivalric romances did not *typically* exhibit such "love from afar"). As Pierre Daniel Huet, the most notable defender of these productions, observed: "The Ladies were first taken with this Lure: They made Romances their Study; and have despised the Ancient Fable and History.... The Men, in Complaisance, have imitated them."[9] This novel emphasis was picked up in England as fully in the "she-tragedies" of the late Restoration as in the so-called heroic plays; and ultimately it was transmogrified in the vulgarized "erotic-pathetic" ladies' novels of the early eighteenth century, such as those of Mrs. Manley and Mrs. Haywood, to create the influential image of a passive and sexless female threatened by a rapacious and aristocratic masculinity.[10] And, as we know from recent studies, it was this composite influence and the presence of a newly literate audience of middle-class women that led to the "rise of the novel" (or at least the novel of psychological analysis) in the fantasies of an effeminate middle-class genius, Samuel Richardson, who would make of its central obsessions an appropriate emblem of the bourgeois world itself.

Fielding parodies the lofty sentiments of the salon romances in Jones's fustian speech to Mrs. Fitzpatrick (16.9), which "would have become the Mouth of *Oroondates* himself," the hero of La Calprenède's *Cassandre*. The endless debates upon punctilios of passion are mockingly echoed in Tom's reflections on Mrs. Hunt's offer of her hand: "But to abandon *Sophia*, and marry another.... Yet why should he not...? Would it not be kinder...? Ought he not to do so in Friendship to her?" (15.11) And, referring to the central and obsessive theme of the salon romances, which a modern scholar has nicely described as "models of neo-Platonic love in inaction,"[11] the Narrator drily observes: "That refined Degree of *Platonic* Affection which is absolutely detached from the Flesh, and is indeed entirely and purely spiritual, is a Gift confined to the female Part of the Creation ..." (16.5). As Samuel Richardson "translated" into new terms for a specifically middle-class female audience the French salon romance (which he apparently knew only from the English vulgarizations in drama and fiction), Henry Fielding, confronted by the novel fact of *Pamela*, chose an alternative tradition and "translated" into comic terms the masculine chivalric romance, which was in essence a summation of the older romance tradition. The comic romances of Cervantes and Scarron, of Lesage and (equivocally) Fielding's contemporary, Marivaux, provided one significant channel of access to a romance tradition that Fielding could not have known in its entirety;[12] but a poetics of the Romance, which can alone provide an adequate frame for assessing the artistic achievement of *Joseph Andrews* and *Tom Jones*, as opposed (for instance) to the sociological achievement of Samuel Richardson, must go beyond the comic romance *per se* and ask what fictive criteria constituted the norms of the "serious" romance as a mode of narrative and as a way of making sense of the human situation.

This is not, incidentally, to deny that Fielding's own "translations" also had sociological significance. The Aristotelian definition of comedy as that which exhibits the lower kinds of men was still alive in the eighteenth century (thus to the classically alert Samuel Johnson, *all* of the new fiction dealing with common life was "the *comedy* of romance");[13] and Fielding's romances naturally, therefore, dealt in a comic frame with more or less ordinary men, not with chivalric riders. This contributed, historically, to the later assimilation of his romance to the Novel (the romance of bourgeois "realism"); but it also made possible his handing on to that new sociological variant of narrative prose many characteristic marks of the traditional romance. Fielding's comic vision almost necessarily "naturalized" the mythical elements of romance, as it also presented a less pervasively sacral version of the romance universe: but by firmly maintaining the essential structure and many of the serious metaphors that had imaged forth a totally sacral universe, because Fielding could still *believe in* a providential cosmos, he also passed on an anti-mimetic (in the narrow Auerbachian sense of "mimetic"), anti-literal dimension of art which can perhaps be seen as having constituted the "artistic conscience" of a genre that through its brief history has had continually to suffer from its audience a strong pull toward the artless representationalism of soap-opera, that lineal descendant of the erotic-pathetic novel. As far as the popular sway of the Novel is concerned, says the capable historian of its rise, "the question of literary quality is not of first importance."[14] This is unquestionably true; and the great artistic achievement of the high Victorian novel, as the best of its modern critics have recognized, cannot therefore depend upon the naive bourgeois-feminine criteria of "realism": other sources must be looked to, if one is concerned with its artistry rather than its sociological impact.

But the great variety of ways in which Fielding's comic vision would qualify the romance tradition and therefore, in a historical sense, "mediate" between the "romance" and the "novel," is—although a provocative topic —not really my present interest, and I have devoted little attention to the matter in the discourse that follows. It is true that the conventions of an artistic tradition create as well as mirror "reality," and hence that a new treatment of those conventions can generate a new conception of the "real"; as it is also true that, if to transfer the workings of (generally) aristocratic romance to a hero of a lower order was inescapably felt as comic, a narrative dealing with such a hero would nevertheless have to concern itself with *his* kind of world and therefore ultimately offer criteria for the "serious" treatment of such a subject. Thus Fielding's comic romances could offer a viable model for certain aspects of bourgeois fiction. But it is the least of my concerns to see *Tom Jones* in such a diminished perspective—Fielding could not really be imitated, as Richardson very fruitfully could; and the significance of *Tom Jones* lies rather in the fact that it is a unique phenomenon and a towering work of art. And this requires attention to its presuppositions.

Those romance presuppositions I have tried to present in very brief outline at the beginning of each of the following chapters, devoted to the topics of structure, setting, character, theme, and style (each of which obviously implies all the others, as I have sought to emphasize by what I hope is judicious overlapping). Taken collectively, my introductory comments are intended to represent an elementary phenomenological profile of what I call "the Romance," that is, long narrative fiction before the eighteenth century, over its whole range. This may seem presumptuous, as indeed it is, particularly since I cannot here present at length the extensive primary and secondary materials upon which my argument is based—something that I hope to do elsewhere in a study of which the present monograph is an offshoot.[15] The term "romance" itself is, to be sure, a relative late-comer in the long history of Western narrative fiction; and, obviously enough, different cultures in that historical span had quite different local interpretations of human experience. Nevertheless, the designator "romance" should not cause confusion if taken in the sense above noted; and if one resolutely brackets off the interesting variant and local elements in the many cultures that have produced such fiction, to arrive at the formal structures and the basic presuppositions that lie behind particular works, certain common patterns do emerge. The Western mode of "romance" is essentially a product of late Greek literature (with only two notable Latin examples, both comic romances); but over most of its long history it is Christian—and this presents one important unifying factor. Moreover, the societies that produced the narrative fiction I call romance, however much they might vary in details, possessed at least three great fundamental factors in common: they all rested on an agricultural base and shared the seasonal rhythms and ritual outlook of such a culture; they were all essentially hierarchical and tradition-oriented societies with a strong stress on *communitas* and *pietas* (do not read "piety"); and they all believed in a hierarchical and providential cosmos that included but transcended the earthly flux.

As emphasis on such a set of determinants ought to suggest, I do not subscribe to the vulgar error that has, more than any other single factor, led to the misunderstanding and misrepresentation of the Romance—perhaps most painfully the medieval romance and the pervasive romance element in Shakespeare. This error finds its origin in the unfortunate ambiguity of the adjective "romantic." On the one hand, whatever its root meaning, the term has clearly been pre-empted in modern literary history to refer to the significant philosophical and literary movements of the late eighteenth and early nineteenth centuries and the various qualities associated with the so-called "Romantic" period. On the other hand, "romantic" is also customarily used as an adjective descriptive of the romance in general. Inevitably, however, when employed in the latter sense it must involve for the modern reader a subconscious (or even ignorantly conscious) semantic link with The Romantic Period in literary history. And nothing could be more fallacious than this accidental link: it is difficult to think of two literary entities more totally distinct and different, indeed antithetical, than the Romance and the Romantic, if by "romance" one means the tradition that I have been speaking of, from the Greek romances through the Renaissance. The *Romance* emerges from an environment that is pre-scientific and pre-industrial: it does not look back with nostalgia upon such a "far-off" world; that *is* its world. The romance celebrates a hierarchical and patriarchal and traditional society, and its vision of the cosmos is concordant: the pride of the "Romantic" movement was that, except for some further sentimental nostalgia, it was resolutely turning its back on this kind of ordered world. Again, although it is likely enough that the earliest Greek romances were produced for "middle-class" readers, as other "popular" romances throughout the tradition may also have been, the essential matter and assumptions of the romance are aristocratic (as even a "citizen" like Geoffrey Chaucer reflects in his writings the ethos of the court), whereas the "Romantic" movement was at its very heart the excited recognition by the middle class of its newly won cultural hegemony. The "idealism" of romance is not intended to controvert or offer an alternative to the existing social structure, but to complement it; as even the most virulent satire found in the romances also aims to correct accepted hierarchical norms, not to displace them. The romance was not influenced by the metaphysics of such philosophers as Descartes or Locke or Kant, and therefore it showed little interest in the kind of subjectivity and "psychologizing" that marked the Romantic age—with, perhaps, the one significant exception of the aforementioned seventeenth-century French salon romances, written to please a female coterie. Which suggests another point: the romance was largely written from a masculine perspective even when its patrons happened to be women (as Huet accurately observes, the romances before the salon romance "have generally more of the Soldier than Gallant");[16] whereas by the time of the Romantic period women constituted if not the largest, certainly the most publicized popular market for fiction and an assuredly influential market for poetry—and the consequent tendency toward "effeminization" of literary (and moral) values, as women for almost the first time in Western history really came into their own as a market and were able significantly to influence the emphases and content of the cultural frame, is a remarkable phenomenon that further sets the "Romantic" at a modal and tonal distance from the masculine romance tradition. Descended from an "oral" tradition of literature, the romance never lost—even in its most "literary" forms—that sense of its narrative origins; whereas the "Romantic" is declaredly a voyeuristic or eavesdropping (without prejudice) tradition in which poetry is "overheard" not heard. And so on, *ad infinitum*: the differences are pervasive and inescapable, and I shall have even more to note as my argument proceeds. The middle-class ideals and emphases of the Romantic movement would inevitably have been felt in a romance frame as either comic (which is perhaps the sole link of Chaucer and Shakespeare and Fielding to the "romantic") or as "effeminate," to use the romances' own term for a stress upon the irrational and the pathetic in human affairs. Hence, to employ the adjective "romantic," when one is speaking of the romance tradition is almost automatically to falsify and sentimentalize one's account: for even if the historian himself does not drop into the fallacy of equating the romance world with its absolute contrary, the "Romantic," his readers are nearly certain to. I shall use the adjectival form "romance" throughout my discourse and reserve "Romantic" for the later middle-class, subjective, anti-hierarchical, anti-"oral" (etc.) values that were antithetical to the values of romance.

All this is not to deny, of course, that the romance tradition was quite as *available to* the Romantic generations as to Henry Fielding; and that they did borrow many motifs and images from that tradition is clear from the superb study, *Natural Supernaturalism: Tradition and Revolution in Romantic Literature*, by M. H. Abrams (New York, 1971). In arguing the secularization of traditional Christian patterns, however, Professor Abrams does not altogether resolve a central difficulty—if God has become mere empty form in a man-centered universe, as his account of Wordsworth and others suggests, is not the continued use of motifs and structures that drew their full and profound significance precisely from the supposition of a providential God's existence also merely empty form? Whatever one's answer to this question, the borrowed modes were unquestionably "transvalued" utterly in their new middle-class, secular (etc.) context; and it remains the most horrid of critical errors to read back alien "Romantic" valuations or interpretations of given motifs into the incommensurable world of the romance. So, too, the particular trappings that appear most to have seized the Romantic imagination (and therefore that of post-romantic criticism) are seldom essential to a generic definition of romance: the essential determinants lie rather among those that I have just enumerated. Conversely, so far as *Tom Jones* is concerned, the romance elements that Fielding rejected or did not exploit are of considerably less importance to the generic definition of his work than the major presuppositions about structure, setting, character, moral value, and the like that he did accept and exploit. Most of the specifically "chivalric" details, for instance, sentimentalized by the bourgeois nineteenth century, are necessarily discarded in a comic romance that is not seeking to be mockingly parodic: Jones does not have to be knighted before he can begin his adventures; there is no lavish description of armorial devices (such as Nashe did burlesque at great length in *The Unfortunate Traveler*); there are no islands or castles or guarded bridges, no giants or magicians (though the Man of the Hill incorporates echoes of both), no dragons or monsters. Tom does not enjoy a cognomen such as "the Knight of the Lion," or "the Knight of the Burning Sword," or even "the Knight of the Burning Pestle"; and the splendidly evocative names of romance settings—the Forest of Ill Fortune, the Tristful Valley, the Dolorous Isle—are unfortunately gone. This is perhaps a pity; but it could not have been otherwise with the kind of story that Fielding wished to tell, and these are "accidental" *not* "essential" features of the romance as a narrative mode. Many elements also that the modern reader may tend to associate with the "Epic" are not to be found in *Tom Jones*, thereby engendering confusion in the minds of those whose definition is ruled by a latter-day collection of set features. The hero's story does not open in the middle of things (as, to be sure, many classical and later epics do not), there is no "epic catalogue" or machinery of the "marvelous"; indeed, it has been thought by the uninformed that Fielding's sole claim to the "tag" of Epic lay in the parodic treatment of elements from the battle-epic: the arming of the hero, epic harangues, the epic simile, epithets, and so on. As I have observed, however, epic and (proper) romance were synonymous terms for Fielding, who was thinking like Renaissance critics in terms of a narrative mode, not merely in terms of "mock-heroic" diction or the various special features attributed to the epic by later criticism.

This central point of view established, there remains only a brief listing (space forbids anything more) of representative titles, which will indicate more specifically the kinds of narrative that have shaped my conception of "the Romance Tradition." The Western narrative tradition begins with the classical epic, although its roots surely lie, as Gertrude Levy and other anthropological scholars have argued, in pre-epic ritual and myth.[17] Various other literary forms in both poetry and prose fed into that later arrival, the classical romance, as they have continued to offer sustenance to narrative fiction up to the present—viz., history, biography, drama, pastoral poetry, essay or prose-meditation, the "character," the epistle, and so on. The Greek romance (very possibly influenced by shorter tales from Egypt and the Near East) is the first long prose fiction in Western history, and may have arisen as early as 100 B.C.;[18] the best and most influential of the Greek romances, however, the pastoral *Daphnis and Chloe* by Longus, the *Clitophon and Leucippe* of Achilles Tatius, and the *Aethiopica* of Heliodorus, are actually later than the comic romances of Petronius and (possibly) Apuleius in Latin and Lucian in Greek. Hediodorus, who was mistakenly identified with an early

Christian bishop, enjoyed an extraordinary vogue in the Elizabethan period —when the *Aethiopian History* was regarded as a legitimate model for epic —and he was certainly familiar to the Augustan Age. With the hegemony of Christianity, the romance impulse and form were at first mainly turned to the production of vigorous saints' lives and martyr-epics, quite in the romance vein; but by the eleventh and twelfth centuries in the West (looking back upon the "heroic age" of Charlemagne and his fellows) a new cycle can be felt in the *chansons de geste*, largely "siege-epics," and the romance "quest-epics" of Chrétien de Troyes and his followers.

The vast and exhilarating pageant of Medieval Romance defies (equally) such capsule summary; but, since I merely wish to recall to the reader's mind some few of the specific works that constitute "the romance tradition," Jean Bodel's famous categorization of medieval romance may here lamely serve.[19] The "matter of Rome" was largely Iliadic in nature, dealing with warfare and sieges (Troy, Thebes, Alexander the Great); the "matter of France" can be represented by such works as *Sir Ferumbras* and the old favorite, *Huon of Bordeaux*. The "matter of Britain," after Chrétien and the Vulgate cycle, would include *Sir Gawain and the Green Knight* and *Libeaus Desconus*, with its theme of *le bel inconnu*, echoed in Spenser's Red-Cross Knight, and *Sir Perceval of Galles*, "the young man slowly wise." The "matter of England" offers such familiar tales as *King Horn* and *Bevis of Hamptoun* and *Havelock the Dane*. The famous *Guy of Warwick*, mentioned by Fielding in *Joseph Andrews* (I.1) as by then a penny-romance for the young, presents the classic situation of the steward's son in love with the daughter of his baronial lord; Samuel Richardson presumably knew the story, at least in chapbook form, for he takes the name of his ogreish Colbrand in *Pamela* from the Danish giant who is overcome by Guy.[20] And finally, the "non-cyclic" romances would include *Floris and Blancheflour*, the two young lovers reared together and separated; *Athelston*, type of the gullible king misled by false accusations against a loyal friend; *The Squire of Low Degree*, separated by his social position from the daughter of the King of Hungary; and *Sir Degaré*, one of the most evocative of the minor romances, featuring a number of motifs that would still prove functional (and evocative) in *Tom Jones*.

From Chaucer to Malory the influence of the Anglo-Norman and French romances would be predominant in English literature. But in the sixteenth century the most influential romances came from Spain and Italy. The so-called Peninsular Romances (the precedence of Portuguese or Spanish versions being still a matter of warm dispute) enjoyed a reign most absolute for almost a century until a changing attitude toward "chivalry," perhaps crystallized by the defeat of the Armada, ended their vogue—few Spaniards, one may guess, would have found *Don Quixote* quite so amusing at an earlier period. Cervantes offers, in the burning of Don Quixote's library, an excellent survey of the Peninsular Romances (many of which were translated into English); and one may recall that only two of their number escape the flames—*Palmerin of England*, because the curate supposes it to have been written by a king of Portugal, and *Amadis de Gaule*, in the recension of Montalvo, which is rescued by the barber: "I have been told 'tis the best Book that has been written in that Kind; and therefore as the only good thing of that Sort it may deserve a Pardon."[21]

*Amadis* certainly deserved a pardon, and deserves better from me than to be summarized; but since it offers a most useful gloss on the persistence of the romance "plot" in Fielding's work, I shall venture a brief *précis*. Amadis is the bastard son of the King of Gaul and a princess of Brittany who had heretofore scorned suitors; the child, committed to the waves by a Confidante, is rescued by a Scottish knight and reared at the court of Scotland, where he falls in love with the visiting Oriana, daughter of King Lisuarte of Britain. Eventually recognized by his father, through a token-ring, Amadis woos Oriana—and has by her a secret son, Esplandian—but their formal betrothal must await Lisuarte's recognition, and, in the meantime, a misunderstanding leads Oriana to reject her lover, who goes madly off to brood under the cognomen of "the Faire Forlorne" (Beltenebros). When this error has been cleared up, Lisuarte misled by Evil Counselors exiles Amadis from his court and the hero spends some years in knight errantry upon the continent. When he returns, it is to learn that Oriana has been pledged by her unknowing father to Patin, Emperor of Rome; and, putting himself at the head of a fleet, he kidnaps her from the Emperor's ship and takes her off to his eyrie on the "Firm Island." A confrontation between Lisuarte and Amadis, and their attendant allies, is complicated by a separate attack upon the king led by the wily enchanter Arcalaus; and ultimately, by rescuing Lisuarte (who has learned of the existence of his grandson), Amadis brings about a reconciliation and his wedding with Oriana is celebrated. The splendor and richness of the full narrative must be left to readers to experience: but the many central analogues with *Tom Jones* should be clear, even from such a summary account.

Although the fact would not be simple to demonstrate, it is entirely possible that *Don Quixote*, far from destroying the chivalric romance (which Cervantes himself obviously admired in its finest representatives), actually gave the moribund form a new lease on life and suggested further possibilities for the treatment of romance motifs. This, in any case, would seem to have been what happened earlier with the burlesque treatment of Carolingian materials in fifteenth-century Italy. For from Luigi Pulci's *Il Morgante Maggiore*, in which Roland (now Orlando) was treated in a somewhat irreverent manner, followed the *Orlando Innamorato* of Matteo Boiardo and then, in the sixteenth century, Lodovico Ariosto's exhaustless *Orlando Furioso*, which of all earlier romances most nearly approaches, in its irony and air of benign detachment, the ethos of the Narrator of *Tom Jones*. The *Gerusalemme Liberata* of Ariosto's dignified successor in Italian epic-romance, Torquato Tasso, is clearly among the greatest of the "siege-epics," but it had less to offer to a later comic quest-romance.

And finally, the Elizabethan period of English literature, fed by all the narrative streams that I have mentioned, gave to the tradition, besides many splendid lesser romances, Spenser's *Faerie Queene*, the *Euphues* of John Lyly, with its ephebic "education," the *Arbasto* and *Pandosto* and *Menaphon* of Robert Greene, Thomas Lodge's *Rosalynde*, and (passing the drama and Shakespeare's romances) the mighty *Arcadia* of Sir Philip Sidney. Sidney's ultimate intention, in the "New" *Arcadia*, would seem to have been to write a "comic prose-epic" (i.e., a fortunately concluding romance) in the mode of Heliodorus, and to interweave the themes and motifs of pastoral romance, with its mixed verse and prose, as a rich frame for his complex fictive analysis of the competing loyalties of love and chivalric codes and demands of state. The plot, described by the best modern commentator upon the *Arcadia*, as following "the romance pattern of disintegration, analysis, education, and reintegration,"[22] is concerned with the physical and moral disguisings of the young princes, Musidorus and Pyrocles, in their unmeasured attempt to win the loves of Pamela and Philoclea. The apparent "murder" of Arcadia's king Basilius concludes in a monumental trial-scene, which not only brings together and focuses the major themes of the romance, but also serves as a synecdoche for that "Trial of Youth" which is the central image of the *Arcadia* as it is the central image of *Tom Jones*. Professor Davis puts it well:

> ... failure becomes the necessary condition for submission to Providence; the hero must be released from all external controls or pressures in order to act out all tendencies to lust, lassitude, deceit, and despair and so come to know his own weaknesses, to trust God to repair them, and hence to purify himself of them.[23]

A better and more compendious description of the thematic movement of *Tom Jones* could not be found.

The decline and apparent death of the traditional romance in the effeminate salon romances of the seventeenth century I have already noted. It is intriguing, however, to see that the authors of these extravagant and long-winded productions firmly believed that their work was more *vraisemblable* than that of their predecessors. Thus La Calprenède (or his continuator) declared in the preface to *Faramond*:

> ... au lieu de les appeler des romans, comme les *Amadis* et autres semblables, dans lequel il n'y a ni vérité ni vraisemblance, ni charte, ni chrono-

logie, on les pourrait regarder commes des histoires embellies de quelque invention, et qui par ces ornements ne perdent peut-être rien de leur beauté.[24]

And the English translator of La Calprenède's *Cassandre* admiringly said of the heroine, "Her ten years story is so artificially [i.e., artfully] contrived, and with such exact decorum, that the truth whereon it is grounded, appears the greater fiction...."[25] In other words, the tales were "realistic" enough to the readers of the age, as to these claimants, who like all "realists" meant that which accorded with their own experience. Fielding himself thought his narrative more *vraisemblable* than that of the French romancers, from whose prefaces he did not scruple to borrow;[26] but he remained firmly enough in the anti-mimetic romance tradition to recognize the ultimate naïveté of "realistic" critics:

> ... for while some are, with M. *Dacier*, ready to allow, that the same Thing which is impossible may be yet probable, others have so little Historic or Poetic Faith, that they believe nothing to be either possible or probable, the like to which hath not occurred to their own Observation. (8.1)

In the English seventeenth century, Milton's two great heroic poems were the supreme expression of the epic-romance tradition; and, although there were several half-hearted attempts to follow the French "heroic" mode in prose fiction, most notably the *Parthenissa* of Roger Boyle, first earl of Orrery, the effeminate mode of romance cut off from the *précieuses* salons that sustained it had little life. Gradually, in France itself, the "anti-romances" that had arisen almost overnight in reaction (*Les milles imaginations de Cypille* and Prudent Gauthier's *La mort d'amour*) began to take possession of the field; and Boileau's devastating *Dialogue sur les héros de roman* of the late seventeenth century (not published until 1710) may be said metaphorically to have administered the *coup de grâce* to the whole short-lived tradition of salon romance, while the comic romances of Scarron and Lesage, among others, would offer a more robust alternative to the fetid aid of the Hôtel de Rambouillet and its successors.

Henry Fielding's own comic romances, *Joseph Andrews* and *Tom Jones*, although they parody many individual elements of the romance tradition, are not in the ultimate sense parodies, any more than Shakespeare's romance comedies are. They *are* romances and both exhibit the same narrative and dramatic elements that had been the mark of the romance tradition for almost two thousand years. Fielding could still vitally and integrally employ the structures and the motifs of romance in his own comic mode because he still whole-heartedly believed (with Spenser, Sidney, Shakespeare, *et al.*) in the fundamental cosmic, metaphysical, and social assumptions that had for so long sustained the romance. As in every period throughout the history of the romance, there would be local and idiosyncratic differences in his own outlook, but in terms of final definition, the community of assumptions outweighs the highly individual rendition.

Both comedy and romance required that the adequate reader or auditor should have some comprehension in advance of the truths that they were concerned to elaborate or for a time invert or hide from the vulgar under a veil of fiction. This has understandably made for difficulties as time has passed and onetime certainties have become mysteries. The dedicated scholarship that has enabled us to recover many of the conventions and assumptions behind earlier literature has, however, also made possible a sympathetic historical reading of the masterpieces of the romance tradition—for those, at least, who find themselves capable of accepting this openness to literary experience that so obviously cannot be subsumed under currently dominant theories and preconceptions about literature and, for that matter, about life.[27] The best that I can claim for my own unfortunate foundling is that it does try to present an argument under the auspices of historical perspective, which rather sternly forbids the invocation of easy modern gods or the resort to a critical language that will trigger automatic reactions of approval in the modern reader. These are admittedly difficult temptations to resist, and I cannot suppose that they have always been resisted; but I have done my best to be unfashionable. The reception of the following argument, however, must ultimately depend upon its success or failure in helping to make clear the total integrity of a very great work of art.

CHAPTER 2

# *Mythos* / Questions of Plot and Structure

The "Plot" or narrative-pattern of romance is normally subordinate to but closely linked with an intellectually (or mythically) conceived larger structure, which mirrors certain *à priori* truths or assumptions about the cosmos. The most important of these assumptions, both for pagan and Christian romance, is that the structure of the full cosmos itself makes ultimate sense, even if the stage of the human world exhibits a dismaying (or amusing) pattern of misadventure and confusion bordering on chaos.

This thematic and structural assumption concerning the cosmos radiates through and connects all the working elements of narrative: plot, setting, character, even narrative style. For if the world of god(s) and men is thought of as dualistic or multi-leveled but also as intimately connected, so too the natural Settings of human action will often possess a "daimonic" quality—an aura of good or evil—that reflects or symbolizes the situation of the actors. And the actors themselves, the Characters of fiction (or of actual life, for that matter), although they operate in a "natural" human frame, will be possessed of a link to the suprahuman—in a word, will have a *soul* that shapes their merely human behavior and in its very nature implies the extrahuman terms by which that behavior will be judged and assessed.

Thus warrant is given for both a "closed," symmetrical, large structural pattern, exhibiting the abidingly "real," and an "open," asymmetrical or episodic plot-action that exhibits all the variety, surprise, and contingency of a chaotic lower world of time and place, ruled by human impulse and self-seeking, the realm of the "actual." Within this latter frame, the orbit of Fortune, particular literary conventions of myth and romance effectively mirror that world's apparent linear discontinuities and arbitrariness: "coincidences" in the action, "discoveries" and "turns" in the conclusion, "digressions" in the narration, and so on. But in the more artful specimens of romance, such useful narrative devices are never gratuitous but are intimately linked with the larger structural plan, as the lower world is vertically, hierarchically, linked with the larger paradigmatic realm of Providence. This is equally true in pagan and in Christian romance, although in the latter an even closer tie is inherent in the theological argument that mere Fortune is simply an aspect of the ultimate Providential order, that aspect which limited man is able to perceive in the world of raw experience and which he mistakenly perceives as pure contingency, unless (or until) his perception is cleansed. In romance narrative, therefore, there is an almost preordained symbiosis of local parts and total design, although of course individual skills in representing this harmony will vary. The bustling foreground action is never merely a sop to the vulgar (though it may be that, too) but an integral and functional part of a more comprehensive pattern. The locus of fictive "reality," however, is not in the individual character or his idiosyncratic actions, but in his *relationship* to the truly real.

Descended from earlier narrative myth and legend, Epic and Romance continued to employ (though perhaps with an ever-decreasing "latent" content) the mythopoeic ritual patterns that generalized and dramatized fundamental and recurrent human experience. Such paradigms from myth and folklore as the Battle of Winter and Summer, the Pilgrimage of the human Soul toward a rebirth or conversion, and the alienation from true Reality, remained among the staple patterns of romance narrative precisely because they were at the heart of what it was to be human. And since romance narrative presents the individual acting out the archetypal patterns of human experience in the world, it can be seen (to speak more particularly of the Christian romance) both as "linear" or historical, like the history of the world itself, and as "circular" or endlessly recurrent, in the sense that all men "relive" Adam's fall when they sin, or are eternally free to choose the *imitatio Christi* or to follow the better promptings of their souls. In terms of the individual hero, romance narrative can likewise be viewed both as "linear," a passage from the unformed to the formed, from *potentia* to *essentia*, and as "circular," a passage through experience in which the goal is one's starting-place, rewon by successful initiation and proof of worth— as, in the ultimate story of man, a final paradise or judgment would crown his long probation.

Hence the importance to the romance tradition of that pattern which Joseph Campbell, working from ancient myth and legend, has called "The Monomyth,"[1] the constantly recurring figure of Departure (or Exile), Initiation, and Return—or, in one of its more significant variants, Fall, Suffering, and Salvation. No structural pattern is more pervasive in Western romance than the elemental but profound circle of Departure and Return (not necessarily to the *specific* point of departure), the controlling figure of the *Odyssey*, exhibited in the narratives of Apuleius and Heliodorus, through Chrétien de Troyes and a multitude of medieval popular and chivalric romances, down to *Amadis de Gaule*, and finally to John Bunyan and a potent number of eighteenth-century "novels." It is the controlling pattern of *Tom Jones*.

\* \* \*

Fielding's structure and his full plot depended, like those of the traditional romance, upon a prior conception of truth in a world where value derived from the assumed fact of ultimate universal order (the providence of God); and he found the romance language of "fortune" and "providence" natural and inevitable as the central cosmic terms of his fictive world.[2] But like many philosophers and theologians of his time and earlier he tended to explain particular events in human history by "second causes," eschewing the use of "the Marvelous" that had been truly functional in earlier epic-romance. Neither for the theologians nor for Fielding, however, did this mean that the suprahuman direction of Providence was brought in question. Nor did the more particular fact that he saw most human dilemmas as generated by purely human failings and foibles—as Partridge's hurt pride and a few drinks lead him to assume the air of a superior man-of-the-world with Mrs. Honour at Upton, and to tell her bluntly that Jones is "in Bed with a Wench," precipitating thus a crisis in Tom's fortunes. Despite critical clichés, this initiation of plot situations by typically human weaknesses (or human insights) was the normal procedure of the romance tradition. For a world *governed* by Providence is not a world in which human action is *determined* by Providence: a central concern of Christian theology even in its earliest days had been to distinguish the Chain of Causes, descending from God's throne, from mere Fate or causal determination of individual human actions. One was always expected to work *with* divine Providence—as Shakespeare's bishop of Carlisle admonishes Richard II, "The means that heavens yield must be embrac'd / And not neglected." The puppet-figure so often referred to in "realistic" criticism of romance is, ironically enough, more totally characteristic of "realistic" fiction itself, with its various sociological, economic, psychological and passional determinisms. The characters of romance (unlike such puppets) possess Free Will, which means that although Providence may indeed place the individual in certain circumstances (as a test, for instance), the moral choices that the situation provokes are the character's own and are his own mature responsibility. His choices can never be insignificant, even when treated by the narrator with deceptive casualness, because they are made within a frame that invests the purely human act in a natural world with moral import that transcends both. Hence the individual's choices *define* his relationship to the larger structure and, it follows, thereby define the structure of the individual experience and the ultimate shape of the individual soul.

Fielding's *Tom Jones*, as I have earlier declared, does not offer in its comic vision a "parody" of the romance structure and plot: its structure and its narrative are thoroughly in the romance mode, and they display all the integral features of the tradition. The particular features that struck the earliest commentators upon Fielding's art were, naturally enough, the "novel" elements (perhaps in both senses of the term) in his "New Species of Writing"; but the assimilation of the new was surely made simpler by the fact that it was embedded in a highly traditional frame of the old. This is signalized at the very start of the narrative:

> IN that Part of the western Division of this Kingdom, which is commonly called *Somersetshire*, there lately lived (and perhaps lives still) a Gentleman whose Name was *Allworthy*, and who might well be called the Favourite of both Nature and Fortune; for both of these seem to have contended which should bless and enrich him most. (1.2)

As Shakespeare's Celia says, "I could match this beginning with an old tale"; consider the first sentence of Thomas Lodge's *Rosalynde*:

> There dwelled adioyning to the citie of *Bourdeaux* a Knight of most honorable parentage, whom Fortune had so graced with manie favours, and Nature honored with sundrie exquisite qualities, so beautified with the excellence of both, as it was a question whether Fortune or Nature were more prodigall in deciphering the riches of their bounties.[3]

Lodge's Sir John of Bordeaux and Fielding's Squire Allworthy share other qualities as well; not least, they have "sons" who turn against each other. But the point is that we open the narrative in a "daimonic" world, in which forces that transcend man himself (Nature and Fortune: Providence will also play its normal deciding role in Lodge's romance) are immediately introduced.

Lodge, however, begins more or less *in mediis rebus*, as many of the epic-oriented romances from Heliodorus on had done. Fielding chose to employ the equally familiar historical-biographical pattern that began with the birth of the hero and his youth and education, then traced his departure (or exile) from "home," his initiation and testing in the progress of the Quest (the search for reputation, or love, for a home or for a father, but ultimately the search for maturity, for the defined essence of the soul), and, after the final and most severe test, concluded with a peripeteia in the hero's fortunes and the discovery of his authentic character—which in the romances normally meant not only his spiritual essence but also his location in a human community.

Fielding's narrative offers a fresh and individual vitalization of this and many other ancient formal and traditional aspects of myth, epic, and romance. *Tom Jones* is a quest-epic (a pilgrimage) or, more narrowly, a variation upon the abiding story of Telemachus—the search for a father and for a public identity—and upon the composite tale of forest-reared Perceval, or what has been called the motif of "The Young Man from the Provinces." Like Sidney's *Arcadia* and many other romances, it is a testing, a trial, of youth in the great passage to maturity. The birth-mystery plot of the hero-sired and abandoned child (already ancient when Euripides employed it in his *Ion*, and revitalized once more in T. S. Eliot's *Confidential Clerk*) and the story of a misjudged "son" of a parent who listens to evil counselors are tales almost coeval with the appearance of narrative fiction itself. And the structural rhythm of these ancient narrative schemes, like the natural rhythm of the comic mode, is most frequently one that brings the youthful hero as close to catastrophic overthrow as is possible without falling entirely into tragedy, and then with a quick reversal of the action ushers in the ultimate recognition and discovery that consolidate a sense of community and reassurance (which, we are told, is the crucial function of myth) and give to that reassurance a feeling of inevitability and universality.

On the other hand, Fielding's experience with the comic drama had taught him to organize his narrative locally in sharply focused scenes that presented the ongoing movement through the dialogue, interaction and conflict of dramatically realized figural types. And perhaps his fascination with the historical and biographical modes, as well as his legal training, led him on the surface level to a concern for significant circumstances, for the authority of observed fact, the "authenticity" of particulars, and, at a deeper level, to a respect for such interpretive principles as the sequence of cause and effect by which history sought to "explain" the concatenations of events. The importance of mere trifles in their possible radiating consequences unquestionably agitated Fielding's fictive imagination as it had that of sober biographers and historians like Plutarch and Livy ("In reality, there are many little Circumstances too often omitted by injudicious Historians, from which Events of the utmost Importance arise") (5.4). This classical concern is, of course, to be distinguished from Samuel Richardson's interest in the non-significant particular for its own sake *as* particular, to create what Henry James would later call "solidity of specification."

The biographical pattern of the Telemachus-Perceval search for maturity can be viewed in very different ways; but in cultures that however highly they value youth see it as a transient phase, important and fascinating because it is a stage leading to the *achievement of* maturity, the rehearsal of this universal phenomenon will normally be seen as a comedy (or as a "comic" romance). Comic, both in the sense that the errors and intensities of youth are viewed from the benign perspective of the adult world, and in the sense that the ultimate achievement after this transitory phase is seen as a socially welcome and desirable end—the whole process is felt as part of a satisfying continuity. Cultures that, lacking an adequate or desirable image of maturity and continuity, celebrate youth as its own sufficient achievement, on the contrary will tend to produce writers who see this process as a "tragic" (pathetic) loss of innocence, the surrender of vitality and idealism for a lesser existence of compromise. There is here a final irrevocable loss of

Eden: "You can't go home again."[4] Each view produces its own typical ironies and characteristic pathos: that of the comic vision may be felt in Prospero's soft comment when Miranda ecstatically welcomes the motley band of low plotters as a brave new world—"'Tis new to *thee*."

> Thus the deeper encompassing vision of the author is in one sense external to his dramatic action, and in another its natural product—and measure. The pervasive irony generated in the gap between is not the savage irony that an ideal Reality casts on Appearance, but the kinder, more humorous and tolerant irony that Achievement casts on Potentiality.[5]

The substantially "comic" view of the serious romances could give a great variety of individual shapes to the fundamental pattern of the achieving of maturity (as well as to the benevolent irony of the narrator). The central interest in continuity, for instance, could produce a tale in which several generations were traced—as in Chrétien's *Cligès*, which is divided between the history of Alexander and Soredamors and that of their son Cligès, or as in the less artful *Bevis of Hamptoun*, which not only gives considerable space to the initial Hamlet-situation of murdered father and remarried mother but also carries its narrative beyond the climactic return home and marriage, to the exploits of Bevis and his grown sons, concluding with his retirement and death. Fielding chose what we may call the "classic" pattern of concentration upon the early life-span of his hero, from birth to the hard coming of age and its reward—the great mythic triad of Exile, Initiation, and Return. The masterly architectonic sweep of his highly individual realization of this archetypal structure, the creation indeed of a new "myth," has perhaps been sufficiently lauded by others; and Coleridge was for once entirely right, in his famous outburst: the plot of *Tom Jones* is a miraculous achievement.

As a student of the drama has argued, the "affective" theory of the immediate moment's emotionalism, exploited in the "she-tragedies" of the Restoration and early eighteenth century, ran counter to such older theories of dramatic purpose as the "aesthetic" and the "providential," both of which required the spectator "to have a view of the play as a whole, for Providence and craftsmanship alike can only be enjoyed to the full when the play is over: the experience of pleasure is a recollection of order in the reflecting play as in the reflected world, in the poet's dispensation and God's."[6] This sage observation is equally true of prose fiction: hence, as Fielding himself more than once insists, the "Design of the Whole" cannot be fully appreciated until the work is finished—the analogue of Pope's very traditional argument in the *Essay on Man* that providential order cannot fully be grasped by the earth-bound senses which do not see the whole, but only by the intuitive Reason. The carefully integrated plotting, the Aristotelian functional unity, of *Tom Jones* is, however, only one among many possible modes of structuring a narrative; an equally artful procedure and, as we have seen, one equally characteristic of the romance when it is presenting the *foreground* action of Fortune's contingent and chaotic realm, can be found in that movement which Sterne would later push to its very limits and call progression by digression. This episodic and digressive narrative movement can be seen in ancient historians like Herodotus and Plutarch as well as in Heliodorus and Achilles Tatius and later authors of romance, and it is perhaps the major organizing scheme of those romances which, like the so-called "picaresque," place their primary narrative emphasis upon the world of Fortune. But we may say that the interweaving of narratives "extraneous" to the central story is inherent in the "oral" mode of romance and epic; and within Fielding's scrupulously articulated and symmetrical larger scheme, he takes full advantage of the possibilities for variety and surprise and significant linking analogy or commentary upon the main action that this tradition had continually offered. What he clearly sought was the greatest possible complexity within a frame that provided the greatest possible unity—in a word, the epic-romance ideal.

Northrop Frye, speaking of dramatic comedy, has said that "in Jonson complexity is teleological ... in Shakespeare complexity is contrapuntal";[7] in Fielding's comic romance, however (as, in fact, with Shakespeare), structural complexity is both teleological *and* contrapuntal. The focused and inevitable drive to a natural end which has been adumbrated in the very opening is clear enough in his larger "mythic" pattern; but attention has also been called by numerous modern critics to the great variety of thematic linkings, symmetrical repetitions, and balanced contrasts that give *Tom Jones* the contrapuntal intricacy of a fugue by one of his great musical contemporaries. If I may be permitted a moment of dreadful jargon, the synecdochic isomorphism between part and whole, individual element and total design, is agreeably perplexed by the metonymic detailing of particulars in all their logical and illogical associations. Thus the tale of the Man of the Hill, for instance, is a synecdoche of Tom's own universal quest, offering in its two-part narrative, as in the famous "Choice of Hercules," two paths to the youthful hero (one, in the first part of the tale, the circular pattern of exile, initiation, and return under the aegis of Providence, the other a circle of submission to Fortune that ends in the enclosed self and rejection of human community).[8] And the tale is flanked by two rescues, explicitly referred to Providence, that simultaneously offer pointed comment upon the old man's story and invoke the overarching force that gives genuine meaning to any human actions. In its *particulars*, however, the story presents a detailed scene of the chaos of this middle earth, ruled by the merely human notion of Fortune's sway, where cause and effect are confused (as in metonymy), where "honor" is a metonym for dueling, and the adjunct, such as dress, is taken for the subject, a man.

But this world of "the Actual" must be seen as inescapably linked to the providential world of "the Real"; and in this union we have a synecdoche of the two-leveled structural and narrative world of *Tom Jones* in its totality. Man's private and self-regarding pursuits in the world of Fortune are seen at cross-purposes with God's plan; but at stroke of midnight God shall win.

In a work of art, moreover, such configurations inevitably comment upon and interpret one another: they are part of the total "meaning" of the narrative. This is clearly true in the structural sense, as I have indicated; but it is also true in a textural sense. Local themes can be qualified or heightened by such synecdochic and metonymic parallels or, contrariwise, they may converge upon and create unambiguous meanings ("redundancy," in the terms of Information Theory), as in the constant reinforcement of our sense that Jones's willingness to think well of his fellow-man, despite all the contrary evidence presented, is ultimately more desirable—though not necessarily more philosophical—than the Man of the Hill's retreat from corrupted humanity.

The tripartite structure (the "magic" rhythm of the triadic)—pastoral paradise, youthful adventures on the road, and the final test in the alien world of the City, concluding with the return to paradise—is not the only pattern that can be abstracted from Fielding's narrative; but it has normally been felt as the dominant one (Fielding himself calls attention to it with a fresh invocation of the Muse before Book 13), and its divisions roughly parallel that mythic triad of Exile, Initiation, and Return which contributes powerfully to the archetypal depth of Fielding's "comic" narrative. There is a notable modulation from the early world of pastoral (and ogre-filled) childhood, a paradise with the usual snake(s), stern inflexible parent-figures and envious sibling; through a transient world of joyous and insouciant youthful wandering that is at once the image of Saturnalian release[9] and a subtle testing process; to the "serious" world of urban society, where irresponsibility cannot be so humorously presented, for the "reality principle" (in modern terms) there regnant offers neither the benign comic perspective of maturity looking upon the transient vagaries of youth nor the mythopoeic distancing of romance. It is not that "scene determines act," as in later deterministic fiction, but that the setting inherently, by its traditional associations, modifies our *interpretation* of given acts. Fielding presents us, in effect, with three central modes in which human experience has been figured forth by literature—the pastoral, the errant journey, and the urban—and these are arranged not only in the order of youth moving by stages to maturity, *potentia* to *essentia*, but in the order of an increasingly severe judgment upon youthful transgressions. Nevertheless, there is at the same time a counter-movement (or containing movement) that maintains the balance of comedy:

The normal action of a comedy moves from irrational law to festivity, which symbolizes a movement from one form of reality to another. The world of tyranny and irrational law is a world where what is real is given us arbitrarily as a datum, something we must accept or somehow come to terms with. This is a spectator's reality, the reality we see to be "out there." The world of the final festival is a world where reality is what is created by human desire, as the arts are created.[10]

Fielding has complicated this comic pattern by carrying the initial world of "law" over to the final portion of his narrative, where it now appears not from the perspective of the child (irrational taboos imposed by incomprehensible adults) but from the perspective of youth on the threshold of maturity (the recognition that "law" is merely the defining boundary beyond which "freedom" becomes self-destruction). Festival, however, is never entirely absent even in the grimmest circumstances; for the mature and benign presence of the Narrator, like that of a providential deity, continuously assures us that we do indeed inhabit here a world of festive hope. And the little domestic comedy of Nightingale and poor Nancy reminds us that even in the drear urban setting of the concluding books an affair which promises pathetic consequences may be resolved in joy. Summer (indeed Tom *Summer*, as we discover him to be) will win the eternal festive victory over Winter's darkness.

The tripartite structure does not, as I have noted, offer the only pattern in terms of which *Tom Jones* could be examined: it can very well be seen as a five-act Terentian comedy, or analyzed as the Renaissance critics handled Terence, in the language of protasis, epitasis, catastasis, and catastrophe (or, as Frye suggests, "anastrophe," a turning up). An analogy could be found in the many Shakespearean plays that submit equally well to a classic five-act analysis or, in the modern theatre, to a structural exposition in three "movements." Architectural analogues have also been called upon, as in Miss Van Ghent's well-known instance of the "Palladian palace";[11] and one might follow out the interesting hint of Joaquin Casalduero,[12] who argues that in baroque structure the function of the mechanical or material axis is to emphasize the displacement of the organic or spiritual axis—applied to *Tom Jones*, the bustle at Upton representing the "mechanical" axis would throw in stark relief the sober emblems of Isolation and "Bad Faith," the negative spiritual axis, represented by the Man of the Hill and Mrs. Fitzpatrick; the positive spiritual axis, of course, would be found in the world of Paradise Hall, the beginning and the end. But, however analyzed, as play or building or painting or poem, the intrinsic unity in variety of *Tom Jones* always emerges. The interplay between the various structural controls and the dramatic narrative provides a foreground "density" of event that offers the illusion of random experience (the prime desideratum of later "realism") and at the same time conveys a higher sense of ultimate order and justice and meaning, which it is the purpose of the full plot to demonstrate and to celebrate.

Every event in Fielding's narrative is accorded a complex significance by implicit reference to any one of the various controlling patterns with which it intersects. Hence any given experience in *Tom Jones* has numerous vectors of meaning—and these may reinforce one another or may dramatically and provocatively clash. This is true of even such a comparatively trivial instance as Blifil's freeing of Sophia's pet bird. One vector would take us toward the controlling pattern of "freedom" (itself ambiguous, as Jones will find—and the bird *is* killed by a hawk); another toward the pattern of "charity," which Blifil claims is his praiseworthy motive; another toward the pattern of "hypocrisy," which shapes the normal ante-Romantic reader's judgment of Blifil's act. And there are still further vectors, as the "deep and grave" debate of the elders on the incident would suggest: "Drink about, (says *Western*) Pox of your Laws of Nature." Moreover, it is precisely this trivial matter, which ends with Tom soused in the water trying to recover the bird, that firmly establishes Sophia's childhood love for Tom: "From this Day *Sophia* began to have some little Kindness for *Tom Jones,* and no little Aversion for his Companion" (4.5). And, ultimately, this is the most important thematic vector of the incident, for the very image of Sophia's bird would inevitably have evoked (for the literate, at least) a world of lyric love. Catullus, on Lesbia's sparrow which had the freedom of her lap, is the ultimate source for Sophia's pet which would "lie contented in her Bosom, where it seemed almost sensible of its own Happiness" (4.3). But Fielding would also appear to have been thinking of Juliet's image of "a wanton's bird" on a silken thread, its mistress "So loving-jealous of his liberty"; for Sophia "always kept a small String about its Leg, nor would ever trust it with the Liberty of flying away." Such analogues are clearly more to the point, in their implied identification of bird ("little *Tommy*") and lover ("I would I were thy bird," says Romeo), than later good-hearted vaporizings on the Moral Right of Birds to be Free, which ignore functional literary allusions to pursue a world of amiable Romantic tracts.

The narrative controls of *Tom Jones* are both structural and thematic; but the pervasive control, since we have here to do with a work of art not a mere entertainment, is stylistic. It lies most notably, of course, in the informing presence of the Narrator himself, the *deus artifex* of this "great Creation of our own" (10.1).[13] As the artistic analogue of Providence, he shapes a fictive world that is itself intended to suggest (and warmly to reinforce) the sense of a providential presence in the "actual" world of human existence. To be sure, a secular consciousness may now, as it might in his own time, question the major premise of Fielding's fictive world, as it also must that of

Dante or Milton—or, indeed, Homer or Virgil—but this is quite obviously a different matter from questioning their moral and aesthetic self-consistency. Fielding's very use of the schemata of romance and comedy constitutes in itself a "statement" about experience, conveys an attitude. It is not an "objective" statement, but a commitment; and (presumably) one need not share a particular author's commitment to appreciate his artistry, no matter how thoroughly and totally they are intertwined for him.

They *were* intertwined for Fielding; and the "initiation" of his young hero depends crucially upon the romance conception of that ancient ceremony. When Jones is expelled from Paradise Hall in mid-winter, to undergo his testing in the realm of the actual, "*The World*, as *Milton* phrases it, *lay all before him*; and *Jones*, no more than *Adam*, had any Man to whom he might resort for Comfort or Assistance" (7.2). But Milton's lines on Adam (and Eve) entering the World had significantly concluded, "and *Providence* their guide": Adamic Jones blithely cries, "let *Fortune* direct" (7.2), and is promptly provided with a guide who does not know his way.

> Il villan non avea de la contrada
> pratica molta; et erreranno insieme....[14]

As Fielding later observes, "Fortune loves to play Tricks with those Gentlemen who put themselves entirely under her Conduct" (10.6). That the man who has subjected himself to Fortune will be unable genuinely to comprehend the operations of Providence is a persistent theme of the romances (illustrated, for example, in Chaucer's Troilus, who can cite only the evidences of Fortune's rule from Boethius but is blind to the argument for Providence). Tom Jones will subsequently receive an object lesson in the distinction from the Man of the Hill, but will not yet be prepared fully to receive it: like the old man, Tom speaks well of Providence but surrenders himself to Fortune. And she will dally with him ("these kind of hair-breadth Missings of Happiness, look like the Insults of Fortune, who may be considered as thus playing Tricks with us, and wantonly diverting herself at our Expence") (13.2); until finally, at the lowest ebb of his pilgrimage, Tom will cry, "But why do I blame Fortune? I am myself the Cause of all my Misery" (18.2); and, with this crucial recognition, make the symbolic leap to maturity that signals ripeness for the achievement of his quest. With this the history turns upward, and Providence fully displaces Fortune in the narrative as guide of human affairs: "Here an Accident happened of a very extraordinary Kind; one indeed of those strange Chances, whence very good and grave Men have concluded that Providence often interposes in the Discovery of the most secret Villany ..." (18.3).

The earliest books of Fielding's narrative had established the filiations that are brought to a first, preliminary climax with Tom's banishment into the world of Fortune—where all must undergo their testing. The abandoned child, in romance, like many of the heroes and demigods of ancient myth (Hercules, Theseus, Perseus), is a bastard for the narrative reason that his is a "higher" blood, as Arthur is the secret son of Uther Pendragon and Roland of Duke Milo: bastardy is often a way of proclaiming The Marvelous Child. (It is hard for the modern reader not to think also of Freud's "family romance.") Traditionally, in myth and in romance, we learn at once the secret, and the suspense lies in awaiting the discovery of this secret to the hero himself or to his parents when he has proved himself worthy of the kinship. By maintaining the mystery to the end, as had the ancient pastoral, *Daphnis and Chloe*, Fielding created a structural suspense of a different order. A mystery, says E. M. Forster, is "a pocket in time," and the resolution leads to a doubling back of the plot upon itself.[15]

The negative pole required of any great narrative (for great narrative tends to the Manichaean) is early established with "the Virtues of Master *Blifil*"—the rival sibling, one of the major romance motifs, from the contest of Thyamis and Petosiris in Heliodorus' *Aethiopica* to that of Rosader and Saladyne, the sons of Sir John Bordeaux in Lodge's *Rosalynde*. Robert Graves has declared that this struggle (Eteocles and Polynices, Esau and Jacob, Set and Osiris, Cain and Abel) has its origins in the myth of the rival twins, the dark spirit of the Waning Year and the tanist twin, the bright spirit of the Waxing Year, an argument I cannot presume to assess but one that chances to fit very nicely with the confrontation of Tom Jones, son of Mr. Summer, and Blifil, offspring of a lady in the Winter of her life, as Fielding emphasizes, with more regard for myth than calendar chronology—for Bridget is only slightly older than when she bore Tom—by alluding to Hogarth's "Print of a Winter's Morning" (1.11). The positive pole, at the purely human level (for "Paradise Hall" suggests a higher positive), appears with the awakening love of Tom and Sophia; and mediating between the positive and negative poles are "the Fathers," Allworthy and Western. Their mistaken leaning toward the negative—the fated role of the *senex* in classic comedy, which is archetypally a celebration of youth and vitality—will bring the initial action to its climax with Tom's emblematic Trial and Banishment. The three major motifs of these early books—the bastard child, the rival siblings, and the young lovers—thus appear to have been conducted by the narrative to a negative conclusion, with Jones condemned to remain unknown and separated from his love, while Blifil, the very image of life denied, is triumphant.

Two of these knots will properly await unwinding until the youthful hero has survived his ritual initiation on the stage of the world and has proved himself morally worthy of his heritage; but the third motif, of the young lovers, remains integral to the structure of the middle narrative. Fielding varied the ancient theme of the Flight of the Fugitives by separating his young lovers and attending to their individual paths, a decision which required the dislocation of straight temporal progression in his narrative, to explain the unlooked-for appearance of Sophia (and Western) at Upton—hence the chapter heading of Book 10, chapter 8, *"In which the History goes backward."* Structurally, however, the most significant configuration is the reversal that occurs at Upton of the lovers' pursuit—for, at mid-point in the action, Tom will begin pursuing Sophia who had heretofore been pursuing him.

This most effective narrative inversion is surely reminiscent of the famed reversal that Boiardo presented in the *Orlando Innamorato*, where in the first book the enchanting Angelica is pursued by Ranaldo (Ariosto's Rinaldo), until he pauses to drink from Merlin's magic fountain of Disdain, which kills his desire. Angelica, however, having drunk from Nature's stream of Love nearby, sees Ranaldo sleeping and falls frantically in love with him. Exit Ranaldo, pursued by Angelica, pursued by Orlando (all of which reminds *us*, of course, of *A Midsummer-Night's Dream*). In Boiardo's second book, the two fountains appear again, with opposite consequences, Angelica now tasting of Disdain and Ranaldo of the stream of love, once again reversing the direction of pursuit. Ariosto picked up the action at this point and eventually freed his Rinaldo from the passionate obsession by a final curative draft from the Fountain of Disdain. Fielding's own handling of this reversal of the love-pursuit is in terms of apparently "natural" motivation; but the mythopoeic quality of the artful romance pattern is not lost, and his strenuous and purposeful emphasis upon providential "coincidence" helps to keep us in the proper romance frame. Magical elements in the romances were often simply a potent mode of imaging forth the irrational in human affairs; and for the vicissitudes of lovers, a set of magic springs or the juice of a fairy herb seem emblems quite as accessible as the pedestrian comment of simple Bottom: "to say the truth, reason and love keep little company together now-a-days."

The middle section of *Tom Jones* is, in effect, modeled upon the wanderings of the knight errant quite as much as upon those of the *pícaro*—for Tom is not really a *pícaro*. Seemingly random, like human life itself in the realm of Fortune, this wandering is actually under the benign and ordering observation of Providence. And, as the "providence" of his own creation, Fielding creates a foreground sense of merely chance meetings and events while at the same time carefully structuring his narrative at an ordered level not so immediately apparent but most reassuringly present. The modern reader who knows anything knows that the Inn at Upton serves as the central structural focus at mid-point in the narrative, with the negative discourses of two slaves to Fortune, the Man of the Hill and Mrs. Fitzpatrick, almost precisely equidistant from that center. All of Tom's "chance" meetings will prove functional in the narrative; but the ordering of events is more total than that, as one can see from a mere glance at the beginning and ending of the middle section (Books 7-12), in which the important opening occurrences—meeting with soldiers and fight with Northerton, Partridge to center-stage, and the appearance of Dowling at Gloucester—are echoed in descending order in the concluding books: appearance of Dowling at the Meriden inn, Partridge to center-stage again in the Trial by the gypsies (a mock-surrogate for Tom's own incontinence), and the meeting and fight with the amateur Highwayman.

The final "London" section brings Tom to his most severe test in an alien setting, of which the "Masquerade" is an appropriate emblem. The formal regrouping (by "chance") of the characters and attendant problems from the first section leads up to the resolution of those archetypal concerns; but not before the hero has undergone his dark descent. And to this climactic event we may devote a somewhat fuller comment, for its significance (and the narrative cues *to* that significance) can most completely be recognized only within the proper frame of the romance tradition.

Committed to the Westminster Gatehouse after his "tragic" duel with Fitzpatrick, young Jones must finally confront himself and his own soul. The traditional rhythm of comedy (think even of the scriptural Book of Job) had inevitably brought the protagonist to his lowest ebb of fortune before the final joyous reversal—"Led on by heaven, and crown'd with joy at last."[16] Or as that surrogate of providence, the Duke in *Measure for Measure*, says of Isabella:

> But I will keep her ignorant of her good,
> To make her heavenly comforts of despair,
> When it is least expected.

The extraordinarily difficult task of the comic author during the phase of "tragical" downturn is, by some stylistic magic, at one and the same time to sustain what R. S. Crane has called "the comic analogue of fear"[17] in the blackness of the hero's circumstances *and* to maintain the assurance that the vision and the promise of comedy (that redemption is no idle dream) will not fail. Fielding, by this point in his narrative, has so firmly and soundly established his own "providential" role that, without compromising either the threat or the ultimately serious overtones of Jones's dark hour, he can astonishingly jest with his reader, suggesting that if he "delights in seeing Executions, I think he ought not to lose any Time in taking a first Row at Tyburn"; and he promises that, if somehow he is able to bring Tom off ("this Rogue, whom we have unfortunately made our Heroe"), it will be by natural means only, "for we had rather relate that he was hanged at *Tyburn* (which may very probably be the Case) than forfeit our Integrity, or shock the Faith of our Reader" (17.1).

The Prison, the dungeon of despair, the image of Hell, had spurred many more romance heroes than Shakespeare's Posthumus to recognize that "My conscience, thou art fetter'd / More than my shanks and wrists." As the modern explicator of Sidney's *Arcadia* says, in commenting upon the incarceration of those headstrong young lovers, Pyrocles and Musidorus, before their climactic trial: "In their dialogue and hymn, the princes show that they have accomplished in their lives the triple subjection they believe in, as they entrust their lives to God, the subordinate parts to reason within the soul, and their bodies to their souls."[18] Even the villain could find imprisonment an occasion for (or an emblem of) self-assessment, as in Lodge's *Rosalynde* the wicked elder brother Saladyne is imprisoned by a usurper who seeks his lands, and "manie passionate thoughts came in his head, till at last he began to fall into consideration of his former follies & to meditate with himselfe." With his recognition of a providential order ("And holdes not God a ballaunce in his fist, to reward with favour and reuenge with iustice?"), Saladyne begins to come to himself; and ultimately we see that "banishment had so reformed him, that from a lasciuious youth hee was prooued a vertuous Gentleman."[19]

Though honoring structurally this familiar romance convention, as we have seen, Fielding chose not to make Jones's regeneration purely a matter of prison-house conversion ("the common Cant of one in my unhappy Situation," as Jones says to Mrs. Miller), for his hero had already *resolved*, at least, to put off the old Adam, and his afflictions merely deepen and illuminate that resolution:

> Believe me, Madam, ... I do not speak the common Cant of one in my unhappy Situation. Before this dreadful Accident happened, I had resolved to quit a Life of which I was become sensible of the Wickedness as well as Folly. I do assure you, notwithstanding the Disturbances I have unfortunately occasioned in your House, for which I heartily ask your Pardon, I am not an abandoned Profligate. Though I have been hurried into Vices, I do not approve a vicious Character; nor will I ever, from this Moment, deserve it. (17.5)

And, although Tom's full conversion is complacently mocked by his visitor Mrs. Waters (Fielding may have thought, not absurdly, of Aeneas in his own descent to hell confronted by the shade of his former love), Fielding means it very seriously indeed. All the traditions that fed into *Tom Jones* reinforced that seriousness: the comic rhythm, as I have said, brings its hero to his lowest pitch, to the brink of the abyss, before the great celebratory reversal; and the romance frequently reached its climax with the hero's last great physical or spiritual struggle immediately before the concluding upward movement. The pattern of initiatory "mock-death" and rebirth in tales based upon classic myth (as well as the related, if more esoteric, dark night of the soul in mystic lore) necessarily reduced the initiate to a state of nothingness and despair before he could enter into his new character:

> And, in the end, to such a depth he fell
> That every means to save his soul came short
> Except to let him see the lost in hell.[20]

And thus it is, if somewhat less portentously (for Fielding's emphasis is not here upon "salvation" so much as upon moral regeneration), in Tom's own *comoedia*. He must reach absolute bottom before the turn in his fortunes that is the promise of comedy and of comic romance can occur. Moreover, if comedy is essentially a celebration of youth and vital impulse, and therefore provides (for a time) the Saturnalian release of total license, it is also in its typical concludings an acceptance of man's social role and of the traditional mores that maintain any viable society in being. The re-entrance into the society from which the hero has been ousted or from which he has separated himself marks the achievement of maturity, the leap into a new character, the rewarding conclusion of the *rite de passage* and the ceremony of initiation.

Fielding clearly felt the need for a shock of uncommon severity to function as the fictive "guarantee" of Tom's rejection of his unthinking passional youth; and he presumably sought an emblem that would bring this happy-go-lucky world into sharp and painful conflict with the norms of a mature moral life. For thus alone can the mood of Saturnalia modulate with finality into a world of rational social norms. C. L. Barber has said, of the alternation of mood in the early scenes of *A Midsummer-Night's Dream*, that "we are led to feel the outgoing to the woods as an escape from the inhibitions imposed by parents and the organized community. And this sense of release is also prepared by looking for just a moment at the tragic potentialities of passion."[21]

> And ere a man hath power to say "Behold!"
> The jaws of darkness do devour it up:
> So quick bright things come to confusion.

Fielding offers a glimpse of the tragic potentialities of passion by conjuring up a hint of one of the most ancient taboos of Western culture, Incest. In a genuinely comic frame it must be (of course!) averted incest, a mock-incest, as the hero's "death" is a mock-death. But the mock-death, as initiation rituals have always insisted, leads to genuine rebirth into a new world of maturity; the mock-incest will here lead to a sure and serious moral reassessment.

Northrop Frye, commenting upon the "comic Oedipus situation" in

Restoration drama, observes that "the possibilities of incestuous combinations form one of the minor themes of comedy.... The presiding genius of comedy is Eros, and Eros has to adapt himself to the moral facts of society: Oedipus and incest themes indicate that erotic attachments have in their undisplaced or mythical origin a much greater versatility."[22] Whatever the root-explanation, there is no doubt that the theme of averted (or even actual) incest was a notable feature of romance and of comedy—though never given quite the seriously sympathetic or attractive coloring that Romantic art would later throw over it.[23] Like many other themes quite uncomical in themselves, the disturbing theme of incest could be treated in a comic frame before the Romantic era because, as Barber has put it, "with sexual as with other relations, it is when the normal is secure that playful aberration is benign."[24] The incestuous motifs in *Sir Degaré* and *Sir Eglamoure of Artoys* and the dilemmas of Niquée and of Florisel in the continuations of *Amadis de Gaula*[25] reflect this depth-situation; and Shakespeare, who had reduced the implicit incestual threat of Greene's *Pandosto* to a bare hint in *The Winter's Tale*, made (perhaps with his collaborator) the incestuous affair of Antiochus and his daughter in *Pericles* an image of that passional world through which only a Marina could pass unscathed.

Tom Jones's "tragic" diction, when confronted with the apparent fact of incest, is balanced by the normalizing coolness of the narrator; and Fielding's control of tone assures us that we remain firmly in the world of comedy. But we have unquestionably here the nadir of Tom's fortunes, the very abyss, the emptying out of the old self and the ultimate purgation and rejection of that blithe confidence that anything good-hearted vital Youth wishes to do *must* be inherently "right" because it springs from the instincts of the blood. And it is most designedly at just this point that Jones cries out against Fortune and then, in one of those blinding leaps that were common to the romance but are not recognized by the novel-reader, asks: "But why do I blame Fortune? I am myself the Cause of all my Misery" (18.2). With this passing of the perilous threshold, the narrative resumes its ordained path—"and that which Men thought should be finished with bloud, had of a Tragicall beginning, a Comicall ending."[26] The return to the world of laughing comedy is signaled by the appearance of Black George Seagrim from the carefree earlier days, by the return of Sophia to her father (Aunt Western having become totally exasperated at the refusal of a lord), and by the Squire's going happily drunk to bed. Normality has returned.

> Now does my project gather to a head.
> My charms crack not; my spirits obey; and Time
> Goes upright with his carriage.

Nemesis also begins to stir, and the Providence that has watched over this serious comedy of human confusions asserts itself. Even the reappearance of Mrs. Waters/Jenny Jones, the very fact that had seemed to threaten Tom's ultimate moral destruction, proves to be his salvation, as she reveals to Allworthy that she is not in fact Tom's mother and that Tom is the good squire's own nephew. In the *Aethiopica* of Heliodorus, old Charicles appears at the final ensemble scene to denounce Theagenes, the hero, for having abducted Chariclea, a priestess of Diana—and by so doing, rescues the lovers from being sacrificed at an Ethiopian altar, since (as "impure" persons) they are now improper sacrificial victims. Of this brilliant ironic reversal it has been said, as one might equally observe of *Tom Jones*, that "we have the combination which Aristotle commends, of the unexpected with the caused; and we have it expressly ascribed to Fortune working under Providence."[27]

As in the final moments of the greater comedies, revelations now crowd hard upon one another ("New matter still?" cries Cymbeline); and ultimate justice is, at the last, satisfyingly achieved. For if there is one theme above all others that marks the romance tradition and the tradition of Christian comedy as well, it is that.

> Il ben remunerato, e'l mal punito;
> E mai no ha questo Signor fallito. . . .[28]

"For, if the truth be known, God always sides with the righteous cause, for God and the right are one . . ."; "God is iust, and will recompence every one according to his deserts"; "Behold that God that euer doth reward / The good with blessings and the bad with paine"; "And holdes not God a ballaunce in his fist, to reward with favour, and reuenge with iustice?"[29] As George Gascoigne asks: "For who doubteth but that Poets in their most feyned fables and imaginations, have metaphorically set forth unto us the right rewardes of vertues, and the due punishments for vices?"[30] It is this assurance and this larger reach of comedy and of romance, transcending the "tragic" cycle of birth, life, death, that has led modern mythographers to understand, with Joseph Campbell, that the redemptory promise of comedy must be regarded as it was in the ancient world "as of a higher rank than tragedy, of a deeper truth, of a more difficult realization, of a sounder structure, and of a revelation more complete."[31]

The anagnorisis and peripeteia achieved, the *pharmakos* cast out, and the lovers betrothed, the members of the "new" community gather in a final ensemble scene, such as had marked romance and comedy from their beginnings; and we feel the full sense of that comic truth, the bitter past, more welcome is the sweet: "All were happy, but those the most, who had been most unhappy before. Their former Sufferings and Fears gave such a Relish to their Felicity, as even Love and Fortune in their fullest Flow could not have given without the Advantage of such a Comparison" (18.13). So the lovers sit quietly, while Squire Western tries to enliven them with songs on the loss of a maidenhead.

Satisfyingly wedded, tying up the final "knot" of the opening books, the lovers settle in Western's family seat, not in Paradise Hall. But that Tom Jones has come full circle in his quest and has regained his personal paradise is unquestionable. Nevertheless, Fielding was wise in this slight shift of location; for it gives force to his understanding that the Earthly Paradise cannot be a static condition, an "ending," any more than (say) the concluding victory of Aeneas is an ending. As Dorothy Sayers, with her usual concise good sense, observed of Dante:

> In the *allegory*, the Earthly Paradise is the state of *innocence*. It is from here that Man, if he had never fallen, would have set out upon his journey to the Celestial Paradise which is his ultimate destination; but because of sin, his setting-out is from that other Forest which is the degraded and horrifying parody of this one. His whole journey through Hell and Purgatory is thus a *return* journey in search of his true starting-place—the return to original innocence. Natural innocence is not an end in itself, but the necessary condition of beginning: it was never intended that unfallen Adam should remain static, but that he should progress from natural to supernatural perfection.[32]

In a less sublime *comoedia*, Tom Jones's achievement is moral and communal. But romance and comedy traditionally conclude with the celebration of a marriage, not because that marks the *end* but precisely because it celebrates a new beginning, the sacramental emblem of a new world of maturity and hope, the assertion of life and continuity as against the "reality" of isolation and death.

The conclusion of *Amadis de Gaule* is also a marriage—indeed, a flurry of marriages, surrounding the formal knitting up of the love of Amadis and Oriana. But perhaps the better parallel to *Tom Jones* is found in the fact that even Amadis's rakish and womanizing brother Galaor, the eternally youthful Galaor, accepts the tender yoke. He weds the lovely Queen Briolania, in the conclusion (and new beginning) of the narrative, for he "found her now so faire, and grown great with infinite rare perfections, that his former loue to her renewed so strongly, that hee, who neuer sought after a woman, to marie her, resolued now to haue none other than shee, and shee with the self same purpose to him. And so it came to passe, for soon after, they were married, and of them descended sonnes bolde and hardie, which conquered by (their valour) many strange countries...."[33]

The romance structure, like that of comedy, wherein larger world and smaller world are harmonized at the last, is almost inevitably that of the completed figure, the satisfactory *Gestalt*, the regained equilibrium, the resolved chord. As Gestalt psychology has shown (at least in a number of experimental situations), the *normal* biological tendency of human beings is to close an open figure or to resolve an ambiguous figure. The excitement of literature that deliberately refuses this normal "solution" stems in part from the uneasiness generated by unresolved tensions. The characteristic pleasure of romance and of comedy comes, rather, from their natural completion of the figure, and their inevitable suggestion that a new figure is thereby generated. This natural rhythm is, however, usually complicated by other internal patterns, and the ultimate resolution of the fictive tension is characteristically suspended until the last minute—a heightening of final pleasure that attends other more homely human enterprises. The total pattern, as "plot" becomes one with its containing "structure," can be employed to subserve many purposes, aesthetic and moral; but perhaps the most typical is its implicit assertion of a faith in renewal and regeneration, for in this it falls in with other expected rhythms of the universal natural world.

CHAPTER 3

# Time and Place / Questions of Setting

The "Setting," or location in a particular time and place, of romance is variously presented; but in general it can be said to bear an intimate relation to the all-inclusive cosmic frame within which the settings of human action have their existence. Thus the world in which human beings act and think is conceived metaphorically as a "stage" constructed by a higher power (*Totus mundus agit histrionem*), upon which the human performers act out the roles prescribed, as one might say, by ancient ritual (the ordeal of initiation, the fall into the world of the "actual" and the return to an original higher reality, the annual renewal of the world and of man, the celebration of community) and, at the same time, make the individual and freely willed choices and judgments that define them morally and spiritually —the acts that exhibit the state of the soul.

Located normally in the world of the "actual," despite magical accoutrements, Setting in the romance may partake of that world's arbitrary and chaotic nature and, like the cave of the robbers in Apuleius, be a place of mere transiency in which ugly thieves' tales jostle with the exquisite fable of Cupid and Psyche—anticipating, however, the ultimate sense-making appearance of the governing divinity, Isis. Or setting may, in such a manner, exhibit some link with the daimonic energies of good and evil that surround the human agent, and thus become charged with moral (or fully allegorical) significance. Or, in fact, Place may merely be place, a setting useful or convenient for the narrator's purposes, or evocative for a particular audience. Indeed, the romance settings are often entirely "placeless," as notoriously in the dramatic romances of Shakespeare; because the focus is upon the human actors, and it is only when place becomes significant for them and their links to a higher realm that it will be elaborated upon and particularized. What mattered was Man's activity: Nature was, quite literally, the "setting," not a central focus or a concern in itself. As Lyly's "Grecian" hero tells his friend Philautus, at the beginning of *Euphues and His England*, in their coming conversations with the exotic English, "it behooueth vs to be more inquisitiue of their conditions, then of their countrey: and more carefull to marke the natures of their men, then curious to note the situation of the place."[1]

Of those settings particularly invested with moral or symbolic overtones two are of special interest for our narrative—the *paradeisos* or "good" place, which the hero achieves after a high struggle or from which he initially strays or is banished (the court of King Aylmar in *King Horn* or of Lisuarte in *Amadis de Gaule*), and the polar opposite of this Eden, the infernal place, whose surrogates—Prison (the Dungeon of Despair), the Forest of Error, the dismal Cave, or even a false Garden—may well mark a place of decision, perhaps the lowest point in the hero's fortunes, where he will undergo the pangs of moral rebirth, as with both Pyrocles and Musidorus in Sidney's *Arcadia*.

Time, so problematic and obsessive a factor for the Novel, was ordinarily treated by the writers of romance in a common-sense manner, their interests and emphases considered. If there were no significant time-factor in the tale, such as the achievement of a vow or the completion of a task (as Sir Gawain is given a twelvemonth and a day to appear at the Chapel of the Green Knight), then time was scarcely noted, or was arbitrarily manipulated—once again, as in Shakespeare's romances. Formulae for creating a sense of the mere progress of time ("with the next sun he rose . . .") had been available from the earliest narrative-forms and still served admirably for a world in which important temporal succession tended to be measured not by unevocative neutral dates but by seasonal changes and by the yearly festivals and rituals that bound men in community and continuity.

The working out of the hero's history in time mirrored the Judaeo-Christian tendency to see history itself as linear—but not in terms of gradual "development" in a temporal continuum of events. Rather, history (of the world or individual) tended to be viewed as a sequence of critical stages, each of which constituted a sharp break with that which had gone before. And this would be of central importance to the romance conception of "character," as well as to its treatment of the temporal dimension of narrative.

\* \* \*

On the whole, Fielding's "settings" in *Tom Jones* can best be appreciated as a continuation of the romance mode, wherein place and time are brought to attention only as they have central significance for the narrative, not to create a simulacrum of life-by-the-clock nor to pursue a sociological emphasis upon environmental conditioning. Yet, there *is* a departure from the usual romance practice; and, since time-conscious and place-conscious modern scholars have worked out the details with some exactitude (as Edward Arber's Victorian edition of Lyly's *Euphues* faithfully tried to do), the departure should be noticed. For the opening books of *Tom Jones* are fully in a romance frame; but the last two-thirds of the narrative can be said to introduce a new dimension. And, although this is perhaps the least important feature that one can point out in a masterwork, the new dimension was "prophetic" of later emphases in fiction.

The first six boks are set, we are told, in the pleasant ground of Somersetshire, with its intimate community and rural sports; but so far as "particularizing detail" is concerned, it could really be any ground that offered neighboring estates and an adjacent village (the "Phrygia" of Emanuel Forde's *Ornatus and Artesia*, for instance). And time—well, time passes, and Allworthy must have been away from Paradise Hall long enough not to have noticed Bridget's condition, and particular attention *is* called to the fact that Blifil is an eight-month baby, but calendar time is not centrally felt as an integral part of the action, despite the headings to some individual books.

However, when Tom is banished from Paradise Hall, to enter the fallen Adamic world of action and of testing, on the road and in London, he also is introduced to what we may anachronistically call the "novelistic" world of literal calendar time. Indeed, if we may believe those who have perused contemporary almanacs, the expulsion and departure take place precisely on the twenty-fifth of November in 1745—although, since this is a fact that one must work backwards with some ingenuity to discover, and that therefore seems more important as a scaffolding for the writer than significant for the reader, it is perhaps sufficient to say that he sets out in the heart of winter.[2] Mrs. Honour remarks to Sophia at about the same time, "consider how cold the Nights are now, we shall be frozen to Death" (7.7); and we are soon again reminded that "it was now Midwinter" (8.9), as we also have allusions to frost and chill. That Tom should be cast out at such a season could not, of course, be more appropriate; it represents a typical romance use of the temporal as symbolic background (thus Sir Gawain sets out in the cold of winter to seek the Green Knight). But, as has been often noted, it also involved Fielding in an odd—not to say egregious—error. For the retirement into the grove with Molly Seagrim that had brought on the notable battle with Thwackum and Blifil must have occurred shortly before Tom's "trial-scene," since Thwackum was still able to display to Allworthy the black-and-blue marks upon his chest; and Book 6, which follows immediately upon the fight, is headed: *"Containing about three Weeks."* Yet all this happened, we know, upon "a pleasant Evening in the latter End of *June"* (5.10) and Tom's trial is in November.

There is perhaps no real explanation for this impossibility except *aliquando bonus dormitat Homerus* or an appeal to the casualness of genius; but one may at least say that it was a happy error. For, not only is each season precisely appropriate for its contextual action—summer for rutting, winter for judgment—but the abrupt collision of winter upon summer most effectively marks the dislocation of Tom's Edenic world, as it also marks a radical leap from the romance world of temporal imprecision into the calendar world of an actual and geographically determinate England in late 1745. The temptation is strong to say that Fielding planned the whole thing just this way; the more skeptical conclusion would be that he was sleepy. Nevertheless, the "error" remained uncorrected in subsequent editions.

And, although it is clear enough that Fielding's plot is a variant of the ancient theme, *veritas filia temporis*, that Truth does prove to be the daughter of Time, I am reluctant to go further and argue that the radical time-leap above described could be an aspect of the regeneration or redemption of Time itself. I shall briefly sketch the argument, but the reader is under no obligation to believe what I myself find rather too anthropological and "modern" in conception. It would go thus, however: the potent disjunction between the "timeless" world of Paradise Hall and the insistent temporality of the world of affairs can be seen as an *allegoria*, an extended metaphor. Tom's activities on this great stage of the world occur in time, in a state of *potentia*, because the achievement of maturity is a temporal affair. But in the romances, "change" of character, as we shall see, was presented most typically as a conversion-experience, an intersection of the transcendent and the temporal; and, however "demythologized," Tom's change (his leap to maturity) is likewise unquestionably a conversion-experience, an initiation into a larger perspective. The conclusion that directly follows is a return to the world of Paradise Hall (the "eternal return," in Mircea Eliade's phrase, to *ille tempore*, to the archetypal Golden Age), and therefore a redemption —though not for Fielding, an abolition—of Time, by "sacralizing" the transitory shifting moment of the temporal through an incarnation of the changeless vision of the Ideal.[3]

Once *in* the world of "time," at any rate (to leave such refined speculations), Fielding exploits the temporal dimension in a great variety of ways. In the first six books he had claimed the usual privilege of romance (cf. 2.1) of leaping over years of no concern to his tale, "jumping o'er times, / Turning the accomplishment of many years / Into an hour-glass";[4] and had focused upon critical stages, *rites de passage* in Tom's childhood and youth. But in the later books a more obtrusive sense of time presents an effective enough matrix or grid for the confrontations, interruptions, near-misses, and the like, which had been common enough even in the atemporal romance tradition. As James J. Lynch has argued, the comparatively detailed attention to chronology in the latter part of the book establishes a standard to measure the variation in pace and creates points of reference that help to integrate (at a superficial level, it must be said) the elements of the narrative and so determine "the unique position of incident."[5] A. A. Mendilow, in *Time and the Novel* (London, 1952), pointed out that succeeding books of *Tom Jones* tend to encompass shorter periods of fictional time in greater lengths of reading time, so that the crucial events of the last five weeks of action appear "longer" than the events of the first twenty years, despite the appropriate quickening of pace toward the end (perhaps something like this could be said of *The Tempest* and others of Shakespeare's romances). And, to confine myself to a single further note, the passage of time is subtly indicated, more thoroughly in the romance mode, by the changing perspectives on Square and Thwackum. Thwackum, who begins as the ogreish giant of childhood nightmare, eventually comes to be seen as merely a fat and blustering sycophant and (in the end) as a fool of so little judgment that he presumes to lecture Allworthy for bestowing upon another a living that he had coveted for himself. In Square's final letter, we see that spruce and positive little man near death, at last contemplating the truths that he had deployed his abstract learning to escape. In all of this, there is no "development" of character in the fashion of much later fiction—Square undergoes a "conversion," Thwackum remains unregenerately himself—but the perspective upon both does change. And, although in literal fact only a few weeks pass between the time that Tom leaves the philosopher and the theologue at Paradise Hall and the time of their final letters, the change in the reader's attitude toward these no longer threatening pedagogues offers a temporal (and visceral) analogue of Tom's own ascent toward maturity of perspective.

Turning to "Place": comedy and romance give to Place an anthropomorphic, though "daimonic" focus—it is what the setting means to man in his relationship with larger patterns that is important. In the romance tradition there are few if any landscapes for their own sake, despite Fielding's complaint (about the French salon romances) that "gentle Streams flow through vulgar Romances, with no other Purpose than to murmur" (5.12). The romance habit, rather, is to see place as daimonic, as emblematic of a world of values at once inclusive of and transcending man. The uses of symbolic setting (as well as character and action) had, of course, been understood by all great writers from the beginning: but they were brought to a high art in the twelfth century by Chrétien de Troyes and by later artists in the romance tradition (Ariosto, Spenser, Sidney), all of whom well understood that the resonant texture of the "actual" depended less upon physical *things* themselves than upon what they could signify for man's estate in a fully meaningful structured universe. There was therefore no particular novelty in the fact that Fielding provided significant emblematic settings for his action: Paradise Hall as the focus of childhood pastoral and emblem of a higher paradigm, the garden and Molly's garret as appropriate local settings for polar kinds of love, and so on; the open road as the image of youth's random vagaries and ambiguous "freedom," and the Inn at Upton as the focus of a transient stage of life; and a recognizable London as the City of Destruction, where the downward path of the hero concludes in the Dungeon of Despair (viz., the Gatehouse), marking the bottom point *and* reversal of his fortunes. All of these join an adequately realized "sense of place" with symbolic reverberations that are universally evocative; and they also effectively contribute to the dominant mood and atmosphere of each major division in *Tom Jones*.

The structural factor implicit in the natural opposition of "country" and "city" had been exploited by the pastoral romance from *Daphnis and Chloe* on, and by many other literary forms as well; but in few of the romances does the urban ground of action receive more than a token rendition, since its major role was to be the logically necessary polar opposite. By expanding the emphasis upon the City of Destruction, Fielding (like Bunyan) found a symbolic "control" that helped to shape his narrative and to enlarge the range of its thematic overtones at the same time that he rooted it in the "actualities" of a society that was coming to find the City both indispensable and threatening. With respect to the Country, as Irvin Ehrenpreis has noted, Fielding varies the normal proceeding of pastoral by having "the country-folk expose the Londoners not by contrast but by emulation."[6] However, the aura of pastoral (and Horatian retirement, etc.) is powerful enough to survive this skepticism of rural purity and to provide a genuine fictive alternative to urban corruption and formulaic existence. It is surely, in its details, a qualified pastoral nevertheless. Or perhaps the ultimate point is that "place" is what man makes of it, with God's grace, as in the two inscriptions over the gate leading to the Garden of the natural World in Chaucer's *Parlement of Foules*.

Not surprisingly, it is in the London world that the factor of "actuality" (what we should call the "realism" of physical place) is most obstrusive; for the urban mode would seem to invite local detail. Not that Fielding would for a moment have wished to provide the kind of sociological profile that later became fashionable in a middle-class urban age: obviously enough, this would have entirely trivialized his larger symbolic vision of the City. But he does insist upon its mundane "actuality": here are definite—and existent—roads by which one enters the city, and named streets in which one lodges; here are doors that are violently banged upon to impress the porter with the status of the person seeking entry; houses that have upper and lower stories (as Paradise Hall itself must have: but we are never told); drawing-rooms in which visits are received; and so on—physical places that are mute testimony to a world where material things bulk large. We visit an authentic masquerade and are confronted with the reality of having to leave on foot because it costs real money to go by chair—and of being hooted at by the chairmen, "who wisely take the best Care they can to discountenance all walking afoot by their Betters" (13.7). We attend a genuine play acted by historically known actors at an existent theatre. And so on. All this insistence upon an "actual" world is less important in itself, of course, than in the architectonic fact that it provides a striking contrast with the earlier worlds of *Tom Jones*—pastoral garden and the open road—as it also provides an appropriate setting for human behavior in its most diminished mode, least representative or universal, most removed from the fundamental rhythms of human existence. This is the world of material and historical "reality" that would become a central focus of much later fiction. For Fielding it is merely one emblematic world and not the central one of his comic romance, for it is superseded, transcended, by a more vital image—the symbolic and ceremonial (rather than material-historical) "reality" of the goal emblematized by Paradise Hall, a world of ultimate attainment perhaps all the more real because to reach it, one must pass through its daimonic opposite.

Paradise Hall itself, Allworthy's "Gothick" mansion, is described largely in terms of the prospect around it (1.4). Such passages are not really common in the romances, although the local detail of an important court or of a joust or tourney can receive loving attention, and Sidney's *Arcadia* gives us an extended picture of the benevolent Kalandar's house, "not affecting so much any extraordinarie kinde of finenes, as an honorable representing of a firme statelines," with an account of the prospect of Arcadia that surrounds it.[7] Although Fielding's description doubtless compliments several of his patrons, and also has conventional features drawn from earlier "landskip" painting, we may suppose that its main emblematic function (and therefore its *raison d'être* for an author not given to casual pictures of nature) is to suggest the garden of Paradise, conventionally located upon a mountain— "Which to our general Sire gave prospect large / Into his nether Empire neighbouring round."[8]

The unfallen inhabitants of Milton's Eden offer only a simple prayer to God and ask only for progeny "who shall with us extol / Thy goodness infinite." So, too, the master of Paradise Hall, viewing the splendid prospect at sunrise, quietly meditates how he may best "render himself most acceptable to his Creator, by doing most good to his Creatures." Traditionally, the mind of the good contemplative man had been characterized as "a miniature Garden of Paradise";[9] and the significance of Allworthy's setting and his appropriate response to it can be seen in such a commentary as that of the seventeenth-century Richard Lucas:

> The Enjoyment of a private Life or Philosophical Recess, ought to consist in Peace and Order, in Harmony and Exaltation, in a holy Calm and Serenity, in which, as in a clear day, from the top of some advantageous height, we *Enjoy* an enlarged and delightful Prospect ... in a calm and leisurely Survey of all the various and wondrous works of God, the Works of Grace and Nature; and lastly in a very intimate and familiar Acquaintance with themselves, and the daily and habitual practice of pleasing and perfect Virtues.[10]

Fielding's own narration, not confined to a single style (as Erich Auerbach's ideal of "realism" insistently requires), much less to a mean style, most effectively echoes this traditional meditative diction in its portrait of Allworthy, to establish "mimetically" the atmosphere of a secular paradisical realm, the center of a benevolent presence. The Narrator is, however, careful to signal his return to the narrative norm of comedy: "Reader, take care, I have unadvisedly led thee to the Top of as high a Hill as Mr. *Allworthy's,* and how to get thee down without breaking thy Neck, I do not well know."

If the prospect of Paradise Hall is the most extended "set-piece" in the first section of *Tom Jones,* the famed banquet in the setting of Upton Inn offers the most notable emblematic scene of the middle section. It is introduced with "*An Apology for all Heroes who have good Stomachs,*" in which Fielding observes that "HEROES, notwithstanding the high Ideas, which by the Means of Flatterers they may entertain of themselves, or the World may conceive of them, have certainly more of mortal than divine about them" (9.5).

> Now after this short Preface, we think it no Disparagement to our Heroe to mention the immoderate Ardour with which he laid about him at this Season. Indeed it may be doubted, whether *Ulysses,* who by the Way seems to have had the best Stomach of all the Heroes in that eating Poem of the Odyssey, ever made a better Meal. Three Pounds at least of that Flesh which formerly had contributed to the Composition of an Ox, was now honoured with becoming Part of the individual Mr. *Jones.*

Jones's lusty appetite leads him temporarily to neglect his fair companion—a calculated inversion of the abstemious behavior normally found in the heroes of salon romance. As Dryden's Crites remarked, in the *Essay of Dramatic Poesy,* "Homer described his heroes men of great appetites, lovers of beef broiled upon the coals, and good fellows; contrary to the practice of the French Romances, whose heroes neither eat, nor drink, nor sleep, for love...."[11] Fielding would later (12.8) very pointedly give his hero nine hours sleep at an ale-house.

While the hero gormandizes, however, Mrs. Waters is feeding her eyes upon a form that, to *her* feverish appetite, combines the qualities of Hercules and Adonis (the imagery of feasting eyes was familiar to romance from the time of Achilles Tatius, where Clitophon says that his dinner consisted in occasional glances from Leucippe,[12] to Sidney's elaborate account in the "New" *Arcadia,* 1.14, of Musidorus at table with Philocles). And Mrs. Waters is also—in Fielding's phrase—preparing to play her artillery. Military metaphors of love's combat, although very popular in heroic tragedy, were of course no recent thing—*militat omnis amans*—and Tasso's account of Armida's effort to raze "that Castle fair of Goodness," Godfrey of Bulloign, was surely well known:

> She us'd those Looks and Smiles, that most behov'd
> To melt the Frost, which his hard Heart imbrac'd;
> And 'gainst this Breast a thousand Shot she ventur'd,
> Yet was the Fort so strong, it was not enter'd.
> .........................................
> Some other where she would her Forces try,
> Where at more Ease she might more Vantage gain;
> As tired Soldiers, whom some Fort keeps out,
> Thence raise their Siege, and spoil the Towns about.[13]

So in Fielding's *Battle of the amorous Kind*," the Graces called upon to assist in the description tell us that "The Fair One, enraged at her frequent Disappointments, determined on a short Cessation of Arms. Which Interval she employed in making ready every Engine of Amorous Warfare for the renewing of the Attack, when Dinner should be over." The volleys from her eye, which have earlier been intercepted by a vast piece of beef, and the deadly sighs, drowned out by the coarse bubbling of some bottled ale, now at last begin to reach their proper goal, and she can improve the attack with designed retreats, casting her eyes downwards:

> For down she bent her bashfull Eyes to Ground
> And donn'd the Weed of Womens modest Grace....[14]

With the unmasking of "the Royal Battery," as Mrs. Waters lets her handkerchief drop from her breast, the garrison surrenders; "and the fair Conqueror enjoyed the usual Fruits of her Victory"—the *quinque linea amoris* that normally concluded a Banquet of the Senses.[15]

The "Banquet of Sense" or feast of sensual love, antithetic to the Platonic *convivium*, is familiar enough from a vast array of ancient and Renaissance examples in literature and art; and even when comically handled—as quite incomparably here—it always carried the same well-established overtones. As J. F. Kermode has said, "The Banquet of Sense represents a descent from sight to the senses capable of only material gratification—what Ficino calls 'bestial love.' "[16] It was not infrequently joined with allusions to Circe's cup as an image of the fall to a bestial state. In this context, Fielding's references to Adonis and Hercules (as well as a pointed allusion to Pasiphaë and "her Bull") become thematically evocative for the literate reader. Adonis, too, is tempted by (Shakespeare's) Venus with images drawn from the banquet of sense, but his fort does *not* fall before her attack.[17] So, also, the famous myth of "The Choice of Hercules," equally familiar in literature and painting (and familiar to every Augustan schoolboy), offered its hero two paths—one symbolized by a lady in white, of pure and modest demeanor, the other by a bedizened female "dressed so as to disclose all her charms."[18] Hercules chooses, of course, the path of virtue; and the implicit comment upon our

Jones-Hercules is all too clear. The heroic Rinaldo, in Tasso's poem, sunk in bondage to the sensual charms of Armida's bower of bliss where the fields of combat are beds of down, is presented with the same image of the two paths by the wizard whose power rescues him from "*Love's* hateful Cell" and "Sloth's deep Valley."[19] And as Tom Jones, happily and drunkenly lying in Sloth's deep Valley, "treacherously delivered up the Garrison, without duly weighing his Allegiance to the fair *Sophia*," so still another victim of disloyal sensuality, Ariosto's Ruggiero, charmed by the visible beauties of his enchantress (and feasted with a banquet surpassing that of Cleopatra, "whose riot rare / To Antony such love and loss did breed"), allowed his allegiance to the virtuous Bradamante to fly from his mind:

> The dame of France, whom he so loued erst,
> He quite forgets, so far a wry he swarued....[20]

Although Mrs. Waters is elevated in the comparison, and through Fielding's own heightened diction (which helps to direct us to the appropriate contexts),[21] we do not, or should not, forget that she has previously been described as "at least, of the middle Age, nor had her Face much Appearance of Beauty" (9.2). Fielding, in a high comic vein, is clearly "allegorizing," as had his romance predecessors, Ariosto and Tasso and Spenser (and, indeed, Chrétien de Troyes), the enchantment that lust throws over the mind in ardent contemplation of its object.

When Ruggiero becomes possessed of the magic ring of Reason, the lustful spell cast by Alcina fails, and she appears to him as she really is:

> When truth appeared, *Rogero* hated more
> Alcinas trumpries, and did them detest,
> Then he was late enamored before....[22]

The magic talisman for Jones is Sophia's muff, left in Tom's empty bed to signify her awareness of his philandering: "Nor could he bring himself even to take Leave of Mrs. *Waters*; of whom he detested the very Thoughts, as she had been, tho' not designedly, the Occasion of his missing the happiest Interview with *Sophia*, to whom he now vowed eternal Constancy" (10.7).

Don Quixote took an inn to be a castle; but Fielding, drawing with equal comic force upon the romance tradition, has metamorphosed the humble Inn at Upton into Circe's Isle and the enchanted Bower of Bliss. Mrs. Waters is the second "Dido" of Jones-Aeneas; and their banquet may recall the *convivium* at which Aeneas ("deo similis" with youth's high color) was viewed by Dido, who burned as she looked upon him:

> nec non et vario noctem sermone trahebat
> infelix Dido longumque bibebat amorem.[23]

The description of Paradise Hall invoked an ancient meditative and pastoral strain in the romance; the Banquet at Upton called upon an equally traditional diction and collocation of images to make its pointed comment upon mere random lust. Each account harmonizes nicely, of course, with the dominant atmosphere of its section of *Tom Jones*: the Arcadian pastoralism of the first section, the ambiguous and transient Saturnalian "freedom" of the second. The same is equally true of the major settings and the "mimetic" diction of the third realm, the London section of the narrative. The hero is here somewhat out of his element—to Tom, as well as to his romance ancestors, the city is an alien environment, the City of Destruction. A doorporter whom he confronts in his search for Sophia is compared to Cerberus, whom Aeneas must appease by a sop (13.2), and this image of the Stygian realm is scarcely accidental; but even such evocative classical comparisons themselves will fall off in the last six books, as the romance envelope of the narrative becomes temporarily diminished. Nevertheless, in a very real sense London is Tom's Perilous Isle, the sinister labyrinth, and the final testing-ground, where he will confront his severest challenge in an alien and hostile setting. He is here the raw youth, the Young Man from the Provinces who, like Perceval, or Lancelot in some versions of his story, comes to court with no training in the niceties of chivalric conduct but with an inherently noble blood. (In some of the accounts of Perceval, the young hero rides into Arthur's court and accidentally knocks off the king's headgear.)

In London, Tom's "natural Gallantry" will appear a diminished thing, aped in the "Town-Foppery" of Nightingale's inappropriately "Arcadian" sentiments (13.5), and perverted in the degrading liaison with Lady Bellaston, a "demi-rep," in the autumnal years of her life. That he should meet her at a Masquerade is entirely fitting (as it is also likely enough that in choosing for her the disguise of "the Queen of the Fairies" Fielding had not forgotten his Ben Jonson). The literary world that is appropriately invoked in the third section of *Tom Jones* is, in its particulars, less that of the romance than, on the "comical" side, that of the recent stage and, on the "tragical" side, of the "she-tragedies" and the erotic-pathetic ladies' novels of such as Mrs. Manley and Mrs. Haywood.

Thus the little tragicomedy of Nightingale and Nancy Miller, complete with financier father and opposing uncle, is entirely proper to the comic stage, and particularly to such modern imitations of Terence's *Adelphi* as Shadwell's *Squire of Alsatia*, Steele's *Tender Husband*, and Fielding's own *Good-Natured Man* (*The Fathers*); and the several "closet scenes" in Tom's bedroom recall again the *Squire of Alsatia* and Etherege's *She Wou'd If She Cou'd*. The vicious plot against Sophia ("the most tragical Matter in our whole History") calls up the other two popular literary worlds, redolent of degeneracy: Lady Bellaston advises Lord Fellamar to rape Sophia and then huddle up a marriage, and mocks his initial scruples, much as the Baron

D'Espernay urges the Count D'Elmont to rape Melliora in Mrs. Haywood's popular piece of "erotic-pathetic" genteel pornography, *Love in Excess*.[24] And, when the impassioned Fellamar finds Sophia alone, she is quite appropriately reading in Southerne's *Fatal Marriage*, one of the "she-tragedies" (this one, indeed, based upon a tale by Aphra Behn) that had effectively displaced the heroic play.[25] When a different "world" suddenly erupts into this fetid and effeminate atmosphere it comes like a breath of fresh air:

> Another Noise now broke forth, which almost drowned her Cries: For now the whole House rang with, "Where is she? D——n me, I'll unkennel her this Instant. Shew me her Chamber, I say. Where is my Daughter, I know she's in the House, and I'll see her if she's above Ground. Shew me where she is."—At which last Words the Door flew open, and in came Squire *Western*, with his Parson, and a Set of Myrmidons at his Heels. (15.5)

Fielding had prepared his reader for the meaner world of the "London" section with such earlier episodes as Mrs. Fitzpatrick's tale, representative of a like "erotic-pathetic" ethos, and the puppet-show performance of Cibber's *Provoked Husband*, of which Irvin Ehrenpreis says, "As a vade-mecum to the life of fashion in London the puppeteer's work is pointedly staged for Tom almost on the eve of his entry into the capital."[26] (It is also Fielding's skeptical commentary upon the "genteel comedy" that had replaced an aristocratic laughing comedy in the public esteem and upon the novel credo of bourgeois realism—says the puppet-master, "My Figures are as big as the Life, and they represent the Life in every Particular"). And the encounter with the Gypsies had offered, in the fall and trial of "the Youth *Partridge*," a forecast of the tragicomic embarrassments of casual "gallantry."

Tom's commitment to the Gatehouse serves both as the climax of the "London" part of Fielding's narrative and as the transition to a larger world of value. The literature of roguery and other lower-class tales had taken prison-scenes very seriously and had stressed two motifs that were to be much echoed in the eighteenth century: the image of prison as a proper setting for repentance and spiritual conversion and the prison as an emblem and foretaste of Hell. In such seventeenth-century criminal fiction as the anonymous *Triumph of Truth* and Richard Head's *Jackson's Recantation*, the "hearty, unfeigned contrition" of the sinner in prison becomes the focal point of the narrative. Moll Flanders is, of course, brought to genuine repentance in Newgate, that "emblem of Hell itself" (so Fielding says in *Amelia* that Bridewell is not improperly called the Infernal Regions); and it is in terms of this tradition that Jonathan Wild's insensitivity and refusal to repent in Newgate testify most strongly to his irremediably vicious soul. But as I have suggested above, there was also a long romance tradition of symbolic and significant incarcerations, and with this bottom and abyss of Tom's fortunes, where the hero first genuinely confronts himself, Fielding marks with

Tom's conversion his return to the "environment" of romance and the resolutions of an ultimately benign Providence. London he has seen as itself a prison and an adequate emblem not only of the lower world but of this middle earth, the realm of Fortune in which, corrupt, vicious, and empty as it is, the life-changing great decisions must still be made.

Tom Jones's progress is in one sense linear—not in "developmental" or "evolutionary" terms, but in terms of a course of archetypal stages in the universal march from youth to maturity, from rich *potentia* to fulfilled *essentia*. This linear or "historical" progress is marked by settings that mirror the hero's moral and transitional situation at each stage in the series of crucial leaps into a new character that constitute the early "ages of man." As infant and boy he is the focus of a benevolent presence in Paradise Hall and its good father-figure; but as he approaches the assertiveness of self that maturing youth requires, he is subjected to his Trial and cast upon the world of Fortune, a radically new being, Adamic fresh. Of this world the tumultuous "to-ings and fro-ings" of the Inn at Upton serve as no inadequate emblem, as the various other settings in the middle part of *Tom Jones* also contribute to the sense of a transient and impermanent stage of existence— "For youth's a stuff will not endure." And finally, in the harsh atmosphere of "actuality" at its bleakest and least rewarding, must come the redemptive turn to the "real," the recognition at the Janus-gate between mere potential and achieved maturity that the world of Fortune does *not* set the terms for human existence nor determine human choices. As one may see the stars more clearly from the bottom of a well, so in the grim setting of a "dungeon" may occur the recognition of a providential order that gives ultimate "comic" (in its Dantean sense) meaning to the locally "comic" postures of the human hero.

But there is a circular pattern also, in terms of which this endlessly iterated adventure—the coming of age—may be seen. The action of romance often takes the shape of a circle: the hero, born in a deep forest or in the country, moves out through the corruption and temptation of the world of Fortune, and concludes with retirement (now cognizant of what the world can offer) once again to the primal reality of his place of birth. The Man of the Hill's story, as we have seen, is an ambiguous commentary upon this pattern. Or, the hero may be exiled from his proper home as a youth and travel to confront the pangs of initiation until he has proved the right to assume his just place:

> ... and there, may all thy ends,
> As the beginnings here, proue purely sweet,
> And perfect in a circle alwayes meet.
> ..................................

> This is that good ÆNEAS, past through fire,
> Through seas, stormes, tempests: and imbarqu'd for hell,
> Came backe vntouch'd. This man hath trauail'd well.[27]

If, overcome by the modern need to know precisely where one is geographically, one should sit down to plot on a map the topography of *Tom Jones* and follow Tom's wanderings north from Somerset, through Gloucester and Upton, to the region of Meriden and Coventry, then south along the Chester Post-Road to London, concluding with the return along the Exeter Road to the west country, what one would have would be a circle of more than mere geographic significance. For, as in Ben Jonson's tribute to William Roe, the figure of the circle is a physical emblem of the spiritual coming of age.

The figure of the Circle can, of course, symbolize many things both negative and positive; but most typically it is the symbol of, at once, a fulfilled quest and a new beginning—like the ancient emblematic snake grasping its own tail. Thus it is not only the figure of completion, of totality, of closure, but also of fresh awakening and rebirth. Tom Jones's circular pilgrimage is this, as it is likewise the circle of Ulysses—the return home after the confrontation with one's own personal Troy (and the dallying along the way with one's own personal Calypso). It is the circle of departure, experience, and return. Tom is changed in his very soul—no mere "development"—by his experience; he attains *sophia*, moral and social wisdom; but he is also, as the image of the ordinary natural man, hopeful inhabitant of an earthly paradise, quite what he was *in potentia* at the first: in his beginning is his end and in his end is his beginning. The circle here is an inclusive figure—not the figure of egoism or of a closed alienation, as with the Man of the Hill and Mrs. Fitzpatrick, but of ultimate accommodation. Its farthest point of departure may prove, physically and spiritually, to be a long way from its beginning, but its curve is toward reintegration, completion, and renewal—for at the end of the long voyage lies home.

CHAPTER 4

# *People* / The Characters

As the structural patterns of romance were profoundly influenced by an implicit cosmology, so the delineation of "Character" was shaped by an implicit metaphysics that parallels the cosmological demand. This metaphysics we may call Ontological, because its concern is for the qualities of "Being," "Essence," the permanent and abiding; and as with the providential cosmos, this ontological perfection is presumed to reside in a realm radically different from but intimately connected with the world of transitory flux and mere "actuality." We need not call such a view "Platonic," for, with the exception of a few philosophies such as the Epicurean, it is the dominant view of all classical philosophy, as it would be the dominant perspective of Christian philosophy well into the eighteenth century, when the effect of competing emphases upon "Becoming" began seriously to be felt.

Reflecting this ontological orientation, the romance interest in Character was focused upon the essence that lay behind purely existential "accidentals" of individual nature, focused upon the qualities that had permanent significance and representative force and were therefore "real," not those of the muddled local flux that constituted the "actual." Of course this can be overstated—for, personal observation was the demand of historians and the boast of artists from a very early point in Western culture (it was precisely this, of course, that led Plato to banish the poets from his Republic). Nevertheless, the original sense of "character," "*ho charaktēr*," was of something which had been indelibly impressed upon a coin or seal, and in Theophrastus it came to mean the distinctive mark of nature upon particular kinds of human beings.

Thus "Character" in the romances, as in the classical tradition of comedy, was normally conceived and expressed in terms of a representative typology (or even iconology) of age-groups, passional species, and social roles. The critical principles of Decorum (a demand which has never really disappeared, but is called "plausibility" in the less universal frame of middle-class criticism) and of what was called "conservation of character," that is, a general consistency in the character's essence, were satisfying as postures beyond brief nature that provided ordering concepts and assurances of continuity—often quite as applicable to the world of Ben Jonson or William Congreve as to the world of Terence. And, of course, representation in terms of social roles was for any hierarchical society (which means almost all human societies before the modern period) an authentic mimesis of the actual, not an evasion of truth. In such societies there was no clawing struggle to achieve an "identity" in the modern sense of social or economic status—that question was normally settled at one's birth; hence the necessary "status" myth was merely one of *mistaken* identity: the shepherd's son was in fact the abandoned son of a king (as in Greek myth, of a god, or in Freud's "family romance" almost anyone superior to the incumbent father). But the search for the central identity of the Soul *was* central to the romance as to the major myths—it was the search for the soul's true essence. And the soul was the informing principle and the incarnation of transcendent value in a human creature existent in a created world (*natura naturata*) of interlocked meanings and higher reference; hence, it was the human soul that was of primary concern to the delineator of character. The "external," "accidental," and merely "existential" features were always interesting and often amusing; but their real importance to the artist was that they served as cues to a deeper "reality"—the essence of the soul.

It follows that the "psychology" we have been conditioned to look for in modern literary characters is never, in the romance tradition, simply the end-product of various behavioral or social determinisms: it is, rather a "psychology"—the *logos* of the *psyche* in its root sense—and the crucial emphasis in Christian (and many pagan) views of the soul is always upon its free will, however corrupted by sin, to make moral choices in circumstances that may not at all be of its own choosing.[1] This is the primal fictive situation of romance: the Test of the Soul on its pilgrimage through the world of the actual. The key to the state of the soul, the "Psycheology" of the Character, is the good that the will consistently pursues, for in his definition of the "good" the character defines himself. The romance view of experience is synthetic, not analytic: that is, human *actions* are referred to a larger scale of implication and judgment than the mere individual motive, because the human soul represents an intersection of the human and the transcendent. Thus, when Chrétien's Lancelot mounts the famed cart in *Le Conte de la charrette*, one does not trivially ask what his "psychological" motive might be but rather what it *signifies* for a knight and a servant of God so to behave (one may well be led to suspect that it signifies the absurd and effeminate power of irrational love, when he later, meditating on his lady, rides comically into a ford: "he knows not whether he is alive or dead, forgetting even his own name").[2]

Again, as I have already suggested, although Christian thought took over the Judaic emphasis upon a "linear" pattern in history, it also imbibed that apocalyptic strain which saw history not as a gradual "evolution" or "development," but rather as a series of crucial leaps into states that were radically different from what had gone before. And this was inevitably generalized to apply to the history of individuals as well: not only the Seven Ages of the World, but the Seven Ages of Man. We, of course, in a scientific-industrial, socially mobile age, are obsessed with the idea of "change"; and, in one sense, so were the romances. But, given their premises of "essential" character, genuinely *significant* change (in the soul) could only be conceived of as a radical leap, a totally fresh definition of the "good," and therefore a new definition of the character's essence. Although the general notion always existed that any change could proceed by gradual and minute stages, the more typical pattern of character-change in the romance is the "conversion-experience," the fundamental reorientation of the soul. Joaquin Casalduero has observed of Cervantes' era that the concept of a gradual "evolution" in character toward good or evil is "foreign to the Baroque, an epoch which is very sensitive to 'conversion' and to the different cycles of man's life";[3] precisely this may, in fact, be said of the entire span of the romance tradition.

And, finally, a "typological" conception of character will produce public and generalized figures, observed from without and distilled—for, in actual truth, "all people are types, and all types people."[4] No one can, I think, read Aristotle's "characters" of the Young Man and the Old in the *Rhetoric* (2.12-13) without enjoying the "shock of recognition" and feeling their continued validity after two thousand years, as representative essences. The same is true of the entire tradition of Theophrastan character, in which the elements that may be received as discordant to the modern ear are seldom the generic traits (which persist) but rather those which "individualize" the type for a particular historical culture and which can be seized only by an effort of the historical imagination, because individuality is always a local matter.

\* \* \*

The major characters, and many of the minor characters, in *Tom Jones* have their romance "equivalents" and, in large part, they perform their analogous romance functions—as I have tried to suggest in some of the later comment upon particular persons. And I should argue that it is in these terms—as notable creations of a literary language, performing traditional and representative (sometimes almost ritualistic) roles—that they are best understood, if one's aim is to comprehend them functionally as part of a total *literary* creation. (The alternative, I cannot resist observing, is to react as do the devotees of soap-opera: "Do I 'identify' with this? Is this true to my own experience?")

Tom is a "private person," as befits a comic fiction, not a prince or even a knight; yet the romance frame in which his average and normal pursuit of happiness is placed links mere individual actions to a richer myth—and perhaps it is more than pure sentiment to declare that every youth *is* both Knight and Quester, a seeker of abiding love, of wisdom, of moral identity. But Fielding was interested, not in the process of *becoming* (his is not a *Bildungsroman* nor *Erziehungsroman*) but in the stages of *being* in his portrait of youth moving to maturity. His concern was not "process' but essence. Penetrating into "true Essence," he said, was the very task of genius and invention (9.1); and he was therefore after representative types. (The poet's business, as Sir Philip Sidney had observed, is to feign notable images of virtues and vices.) Fielding was speaking as a follower of the long typological tradition when he declared in *Joseph Andrews* that "I describe not Men, but Manners; not an Individual, but a Species" (3.1). Thus, too, Samuel Johnson's highest praise for Shakespeare was that "in the writings of other poets a character is too often an individual; in those of Shakespeare it is commonly a species."[5] Which means, of course, that Johnson was paying Shakespeare the compliment of reading him in terms of the dramatist's own literary tradition, a compliment he has but seldom received.

Fielding, however, went on immediately to say, in the passage from *Joseph Andrews*: "Perhaps it will be answered, Are not the Characters then taken from Life? To which I answer in the Affirmative; nay, I believe I might aver, that I have writ little more than I have seen" (3.1). As I have already indicated, this does not at all represent a departure from the reigning habit of romance artists, who drew from the life but perceived experience through the universalizing glass of type and essence. What did strike some of Fielding's contemporaries as unusual was that he employed romance techniques to describe truly observed "low" personages and settings. Lady Luxborough, something of a rustic but schooled in the French salon romances, complained that " in the adventures that happen, I think he produces personages but *too like* those one meets with in the world"; and Richardson, scrabbling after a gentility forever closed to him, sneered, "His brawls, his jarrs, his gaols, his spunging-houses, are all drawn from what he has seen and known."[6] This dispraise became the praise of a later day, during the vogue of "external realism"; but the "anti-realists" of that same time frequently echoed the charge that had been made against Ben Jonson—namely, that he was *merely* an observer, who drew what he saw without "heightening" it.[7] This is an odd thing to say of Jonson: it is even odder to say of Fielding. For what he had actually done, of course, was to reshape—to *stylize*—observed reality in the service of a more vital artistic and moral truth than raw experience as such could offer; and the schemata (the glasses) through which he apprehended and ordered this personal experience of observed fact were those of the comic and romance traditions.

Comedy, as it has its own proper structure and drive, has also its own proper modes of characterization, which are readily assimilated to the mythopoeic romance conventions. Dorothy Van Ghent sensibly observed of *Tom Jones*, "It is well for us ... to bear in mind the generic characteristics of the comic mode, and the fact that the characters in comedy may remain relatively static while the broad social panorama of comedy need not for that reason be lacking in seriousness and depth of significance."[8] (That this should even need to have been *said* about the high and profound tradition of comedy offers a pungent commentary upon the depths to which a piddling *petit bourgeois* ideal of sober and genteel "seriousness" had brought us.) In arts that depend upon activity in time, however, a perfectly static field would convey no "information": something must be moving. The moving factor in the Victorian-Edwardian novel came to be the "development" or "evolution" of the character or of his moral consciousness, and this may be thought of as essential to that particular fiction's vision of experience. But a focus upon "development" or, indeed, a detailed concern with "psychological" particulars is not only foreign to the ontological metaphysics of romance and comedy but would inevitably compromise *their* vision of experience. Even the merest approach to such latter-day "novelistic" concerns will shift the proper vision of comedy or romance to that of the "ironic" mode, which is utterly at war with the kind of ending natural to comedy and makes it appear "artificial" in the naughty sense of the word. Hence (to return to the moving factor) what "moves" in proper comedy or romance is the set of circumstances in which the representative and typological characters, the necessary points of stable reference by which alone we can judge "movement," are involved. The movement of circumstances (the "Plot") generates meaningful patterns that transcend the individuals who act them out.

One should therefore not expect to find "development," in the later gradualist sense, of characters in *Tom Jones* or in any other romance. Neither the conventions of comedy nor those of romance found, for their aims, such a primary accent upon the temporal flux desirable or significant. There could be, however, particularly in the longer span of the romance, a process of moral "education," if thought of as a series of discrete stages, a movement from mere *potentia* to full *essentia*, from possibility to achievement. The ultimate "change" was a radical and fundamental change, as initiation rituals have always insisted, and it marked "a new life," a new state of the soul and of being. This is the pattern that we find in the comedic Rake's Progress of young Tom Jones, from youthful potential to achieved essence and maturity—and the great "change," when it comes, is not a development but a leap.

There is perhaps nothing more difficult (and thus more necessary) for the modern reader of romance to accept than the Conversion-Experience, despite the fact that its occurrence in the actual world of human affairs is unquestionable. Once again, as with the prejudice against "coincidence," a modern literary (or outmoded "scientific") convention is stronger than the actualities of life.[9] However, it is not too much to say that the very image and model of significant "change" in character, at least toward the good, was in the romance tradition Conversion, not development or "evolution." (Evil, it is true, was frequently seen, when not radical or inherent, as a *gradual* distortion in the soul, a "hardening" of heart.) The change, moreover, was never merely "psychological," or behavioral, as we tend to conceive character change: it was a change in the character's "*psyche*ology," a reorientation of the *soul*. It did not seek to be "natural," for in fact it was not (*natura non facit saltum*), it was spiritual and transcendent; and, although such a spiritual change could well be prepared for by a series of steps,[10] the moment of conversion itself was more typically an instantaneous phenomenon:

> Consideration like an angel came
> And whipp'd th' offending Adam out of him.[11]

Shakespeare found nothing "unbelievable" in this radical leap of Prince Hal, nor in the sudden repentance of Proteus and the equally sudden forgiveness of Valentine, in *Two Gentlemen of Verona*; but it is true that by Fielding's time the "convention" was on its way to becoming merely a literary rather than a spiritual fact, and he himself felt the need to criticize that easy reformation of the rake in modern comedies, which occurs for no better reason "than because the Play is drawing to a Conclusion" (8.1). When he came to the representation of his own hero's leap, however, from rattle-brained rogue to the maturity alone worthy of Sophia, it was almost necessarily displayed in terms of the traditional conversion experience, for only thus could the ontological guarantee of a full and radical change in the hero's *soul* be bodied forth. In this, Fielding was assuming a tradition of ancient date to give fictive authority and conviction to the regenerate spirit of his offending hero:

> He made a blushing cital of himself,
> And chid his truant youth with such a grace
> As if he mast'red there a double spirit
> Of teaching and of learning *instantly*.[12]

This moral rebirth after a symbolic death or "descent to Hell," familiar to romance, was sometimes effectively signalized by the hero's recognition that Providence, not mere Fortune, governed the affairs of men (as, conversely, the failure of Chrétien's Lancelot to recognize this, when imprisoned in Meleagant's tower, signals his moral emptiness and submission to Fortune). Tom Jones's truest anagnorisis and peripeteia—of the soul, not of his external condition—occur when he is able to blame himself, not Fortune, for his misery and to turn with confidence to "Reliance on a Throne still greatly superior; which will, I am certain, afford me all the Protection I merit" (17.9).

If comedy cannot deal obsessively with "development" or with the so-called "inner life" (which in its modern sense has nothing to do with the soul) without ceasing to be comedy, and myth or romance cannot descend to psychologizing without ceasing to be mythical, yet as literary forms they can quite obviously provide an illumination of human experience and human character that is as "serious" and as profound as that of any literary form known to the world of art. Both comedy and romance are vitally responsive to basic human needs; and both inevitably figure forth a morally charged universe. Henry Fielding perfectly well understood the psychological phenomena to which we have given such names as "rationalization," "projection," and the like: *Tom Jones* is full of "Freudian" insights that any reader will note. But Fielding's conception of character necessarily made of these behavioral mechanisms *moral* acts for which the individual was responsible and which gave cues to the state of his soul. It is true that he did conceive of certain involuntary responses that were not in one's control (such as laughing when a well-dressed man tumbles in the dirt) : "but as this is one of those first, and as it were, spontaneous Motions of the Soul, which few, as I have said, attend to, and none can prevent; so it doth not properly constitute the Character."[18] That is, a true *Character* is to be conceived in terms only of those things for which one can be held morally responsible; purely spontaneous "Motions of the Soul" are morally insignificant.

Fielding's interest in responsible human character operating in the world of the "actual" was rooted, then, in a conception of "psycheology" that asked what fundamental orientation of the soul (this would be transformed as Hume's "durable principles of mind") motivated the person in his movement toward his own *telos* and in his relationships with other persons and, inevitably, with the cosmos and his God (the world of the "real"). This is not at all the same thing as the Johnson-Shadwell idea of "humours" or the concept of the ruling passion (although Fielding found both of these interesting—as they are) : it is, rather, the kind of ontological question asked about character by Virgil, by Chrétien de Troyes, by Ariosto, by Spenser or Milton; in a word, it is the fundamental mode of characterization that one finds in the epic-romance tradition. Within this metaphysical and moral frame, however, there is room for the greatest variety and depth and subtlety that genius can command. Nuance of character-drawing is no more a unique preserve of latter-day art than is nuance of symbolic configuration; but the nuances of character in the romance and in comedy are likely to occur within a recognizable type-outline, as the inexhaustible freshness of

Falstaff is recognizably elaborated within the frame of the medieval "Vice" figure which carries the primary significance of his relationship to young Prince Hal. One high achievement of the romance tradition is to have created archetypal figures who remain true to generalized human experience, transcending variations in local cultural detail, but who are nevertheless rendered in terms of personal idiosyncrasies that make them unique beings. There is no one else in all of literature who could really be confused with Squire Western. And, surprisingly, for his "overt" characterization at first seems slight and his "function" is to be representative of the *adulescens*, there is not really another Tom Jones.

Another aspect of the typological view of literary character is that character tends to be conceived in terms of and expressed in the language of social roles.[14] The emphasis in romance falls upon the "public" dimension and significance of character, even when the personage is not of exalted stature, rather than the "private" world of domestic relationships and the "inner life." The conventions for dealing with internal debate and the like (the soliloquy, the *intestinum bellum*) were aimed at making essentially private matters, of no concern to anyone but the individual himself, "public" and accessible in the most universal terms. Literary character could also be given such a public and general dimension by allusions that metaphorically placed it in a tradition or continuity and that (incidentally) thereby also made its individual elements the more striking. Tom Jones's "character" is better conceived in terms of his "public" role as *adulescens* and of the typological and allusive roles (Adam, Aeneas, Adonis, and so on), which place him in a tradition of *literary* character, than in modern terms of non-fictive individualist psychology—a language that does not adequately "translate" or "decode" the language of which romance characters are made and within whose ambience they "live."

Allied with role is the concept of social "field." Modern studies have exhibited renewed interest in what had once been a central characterological focus, namely, the emphasis upon persons in a context and their "public" responses to the web of relationships in which any social being was inherently involved. Just as one instance of the kind of appropriateness to literary questions that I mean: when Allworthy thinks he is dying, what Fielding (like Shakespeare with John of Gaunt's death-bed scene in *Richard II*) focuses upon is not at all Allworthy's "inner feelings" and private concerns, but rather the complex "field" of interreactions, expectations, role-playing, and the like, that this central situation evokes. And so with many other scenes in his romance. The social sciences are today painfully reconstructing, on a somewhat different base of assumptions, the ways of viewing human experience that were altogether natural to the generations which saw man as intrinsically a social being possessed of a soul not as an island unto himself possessed of a personality. To the romance world, the isolate from society, unless his gaze was fixed upon a higher "reality," was simply not a true "person": for character and society were complementary and mutually defining.

The romance world was thus one in which shared and public values and modes of judgment sustained the individual in his own identity and in his moral persistence in the right when his own conscience( the modern phrase would be "internalized norms") told him he was in the path of the good. But reputation or "honor" was nevertheless a matter of public validation, and therefore the opinion of others—even of the despised "vulgar"—was of vital, if ambiguous, importance.[15] Apodictically, the greater the variety of possible realms of judgment within a society, the greater the anxiety over "right" behavior and the validation of public assent (it has been said that when the modern American wishes to know what is morally right, he takes a public-opinion poll). Hence Fielding, at midpoint in a slow war of attrition through which aristocratic "shame" judgments were displaced by middle-class "guilt" judgments, displays a heightened consciousness of the importance of Opinion, of the various possible constructions that may be put upon honest (or dishonest) behavior. Throughout *Tom Jones* the obsessive imagery of the "light" in which an act is seen, the "colors" in which it is interpreted, provides a central controlling metaphor, expressive of man's ambiguous communal existence and (therefore) of the necessity for *prudentia*, a schooled moral judgment, that ultimately represents—as one famous eighteenth-century document put it—a decent respect for the opinions of mankind.

Motivation is another element in the rendition of "character" that is subject to changes in taste and fashion: Fielding criticized the lack of motivation and probability in the French salon romances, just as later perspectives would criticize what they found to be a lack of motivation (as newly and "mechanically" understood) in his own. There is a difference, however, between mere plausibility (local decorum) and a sense of inevitability—a difference evident, in fact, in all the great novels of the nineteenth century. Fielding's characters, like those of the romance tradition generally, are motivated at a number of levels, from the very practical and personal motives of Partridge, who is looking for ultimate profit, to the almost "unmotivated" malice of Blifil, felt as a mere force of nature. Yet Blifil, like Iago, is true to our "essential" not "existential" intuitions of human character, as he is also true to the intuitions of myth. Moreover, in terms of literary structure, a Blifil or an Iago (both surrounded by imagery of the Devil) provides a fixed point about which more complicated, if not more complex, motivations may pivot. Blifil is the opposing force which, like mere nature itself, does not always answer to "plausible" expectations, and which therefore generates in the reader a strong countermovement toward the implicit *human* norm.

Fielding's characters express themselves and their motives not only through the actual language of the day but also through rhetorical conventions of language and gesture that lift their communications to a more universal level. An extreme but not an atypical instance would be Allworthy's sage exhortation to the "erring" Jenny Jones, a formal and classical oration possessing the recognized *partes* (exordium, narratio, divisio, confirmatio, refutatio, and peroratio) recommended by Quintilian, and underscoring functionally in its very structure and diction the rather old-fashioned formal quality of Allworthy's kindly but fallible wisdom. Lesser rhetorics were also at hand: although Fielding did not accept John Locke's nominalistic emphasis, the Lockeian concentration upon the process of the mind in coming to terms with a reality "out there" unquestionably did influence his own *vocabulary* for dealing with mental events and provided him (as it would more unreservedly provide the "novel") with a surface rhetoric that had not been accessible in the same terms to the romance tradition.

The more familiar rhetorical conventions of the law and of popular casuistry[16] offered a focus upon the "circumstances" of moral actions and the state of conscience of the person involved, that gave the narrator as well as his characters a recognizable and satisfying language for assessing motive. When Fielding comments upon Jones's retirement into the grove with Molly Seagrim, it is to contrast legal judgment with the casuistic plea *in foro conscientiae*: "in a Court of Justice, Drunkenness must not be an Excuse, yet in a Court of Conscience it is greatly so" (5.10);[17] and the learned Square will typically abuse the legitimate aims of casuistry and of equity by citing their basic argument, when caught *in flagrante* with Molly: "For you must know, Mr. *Jones*, in the Consideration of Fitness, very minute Circumstances, Sir, very minute Circumstances cause great Alteration" (5.5).

Fielding's characters exist, then, in a web of language or, to vary the figure, are surrounded by a penumbra of language; and to abstract them from this very source of their being in order to "analyze" them after latter-day dogmas can only be like a very bad and very flat translation of a very good poem. It is true enough that any historically existent construct of words may serve as a set of "cues" to fresh and novel inference: Robert Alter has, for instance, recently examined in contemporary terms some of the ways in which Fielding's "shrewdly reticent presentation of details of characterization invites us to reconstruct character by inference, just as the cues for his verbal irony invite us to summon up a sustained alertness as readers in order to revise and reconstruct verbal meanings."[18] In good hands, this process of inferring can be an exhilarating exercise; but one does well to remember that the characters of romance, like the characters of comedy, never exist as isolated "psychological" beings—they inevitably take their shape and their ontological status from the fact that they are integral members of significant worlds (including language worlds) and of significant wholes that are larger than themselves.

Tom Jones as a character has, as I have remarked, one primary function: he is The Young Man (not merely *a* young man, as the novel's focus would demand, a particular young man with a particular "psychology" and "personality"); but he is also The Hero, who (in any era) is a projection of the eternal desire that what we conceive to be "truth and right" should prevail. Tom Jones is a genuinely representative figure, and representative figures do not get their full dimension from local particularities: dimension comes from tradition and from a complete artistic realization by the individual author of the qualities and experiences attributed to a given figure in that tradition. It is not only, as Henry James said in his generous tribute to Fielding in the preface to *The Princess Casamassima*, that Tom is given "amplitude of reflexion" through Fielding's own richness of mind; but also that, in evoking the whole sweep of the epic-romance tradition and of the myths and rituals that lay behind it, Fielding vastly amplified the fictive significance of Tom's elemental career. As has been said of Don Quixote, Tom Jones's every act is an allusion.

If bastardy in myth and legend was a way of proclaiming the marvelous child, set apart for some representative deed, it also marked the Outsider, whose ambiguous relationship to his society urgently required him to define himself, and whose free agency (as it were) also gave him a peculiar license to test and define the codes of his society: thus Tom's actions, for instance, will more than once offer an implicit questioning of the code of "honor" in his world. And Tom's bastardy also served Fielding in another related manner: for the representation of Youth was the representation of pure potential, as yet unfixed in the determinate essence of maturity; and a bastard with no acknowledged heritage could, in one sense, most fully embody the young man who is entirely *potentia*. Little space is devoted to Tom's childhood; for the romance, unlike the "Romantic" child-centered mode, was primarily interested in characters who could be considered responsible for their actions; and the youthful periods of genuine interest were those of the *rites de passage*, such as the time of puberty (when the young hero, like Tristram or Perceval or Palmerin d'Oliva, begins to testify by his delight in hunting and other manly exercises that he is of true chivalric temper) and the approach to manhood and the ceremony of initiation.

Fielding's narrative faithfully pursues these emphases, although as always his realization of the archetypal situations is his own; and he could playfully invert some of them. For instance, the advent of the hero, in myth as in romance, was very often marked by impressive omens and prophecies: thus Merlin tells Uther Pendragon that his secret son will be king of the land,

and the enchantress Urganda the Unknown prophesies that Amadis will one day be the flower of chivalry. As for little Tommy Jones, honesty compels his historian to acknowledge "even at his first Appearance, that it was the universal Opinion of all Mr. *Allworthy's* Family, that he was certainly born to be hanged" (3.2). To alert us to the proper context, the chapter-heading reads: *"The Heroe of this great History appears with very bad Omens."*

To pass over the hero's relationship to such figures as the rival sibling, which I have already briefly touched upon, and his tutors and other father-figures, we may come to Tom as the young lover of an eminently lovable Sophia, who is introduced with all the splendid resonance traditional to romance. Sophia, as heroine, might say to Western what Imogen tells her father:

> It is your fault that I have lov'd Posthumus.
> You bred him as my playfellow, and he is
> A man worth any woman. . . .

But if this theme of playmates in an Arcadian world (Floris and Blancheflour) is familiar in romance, so too is the gulf between the lovers created by the ambiguity of the hero's birth or status (Guy of Warwick, the Squire of Low Degree, Amadis); and, in despair, our young man of high "animal spirits" turns to an inappropriate substitute. Molly Seagrim has the sexual forthrightness of the Saracen and other pagan princesses who, like Josian in *Bevis of Hamptoun*, can assure the hero that they would prefer his naked body to all the gifts of "Mahoun"; but she is also, as Fielding reminds us (5.10) with a lovely allusion to the fourth book of the *Aeneid*, the equivalent of Dido for Jones-Aeneas, who must ultimately be put off for a higher love, although there will also be, unfortunately, other Dido's—"alter habendus amor tibi restat et altera Dido"[19]—before Tom can close with his proper Lavinia.

Betrayed by Blifil and the Evil Counselors of romance, Thwackum and Square, the youthful hero undergoes his trial and banishment, his Exile from the *paradeisos*, and his leap into a new stage of existence. The "violent Agonies," incidentally, into which Tom falls when he has thrown himself down by a brook (6.12), like other "fits of madness" in which he will indulge, gain their resonance from the long *furioso* tradition (the wrath of Achilles, the madness of Ajax, Hercules *furens*), which in the romances served as an emblem of the triumph of the lower effeminate passions over the masculine reason, reducing man to a level with the merely animal—a condition that was never considered, as in the Romantic perspective, cause for celebration. The madness of Chrétien's Yvain, of Lancelot and Tristram and Partonope of Blois, of Ariosto's Orlando and of Amadis, among others, dramatically declared this fatal and effeminate weakness in man—most notably and peculiarly (and comically) in the delirium of irrational love. And it is precisely this intemperance and irrationality and immature fire in Jones, for which the romance tradition provided such speaking images, that must ultimately be brought under the sway of a hard-earned moral wisdom (*sophia*).

In the world of Fortune where his testing must take place, Jones does not properly behave like a bourgeois hero with a living to make (which has understandably disturbed some of his critics), but rather like a knight errant, who proffers his services to the soldiers of a righteous cause, as banished Amadis offers to join in King Tafinor's campaign against the invading emperor of Rome. Like any knight, Tom takes a squire, who like other romance squires is often berated for not chiming with his master's mood or drubbed for his misdeeds, but who also (like the *servus* of Roman comedy) acts as a furtherer of the plot. And the hero finds, as he pursues his errant path, that his "reputation" has preceded him—although in his case, not the deeds of the Knight of the Green Sword, but, rather, the wide-ranging scandal that he has been "turned out of Doors" (8.8). He meets with "*a very extraordinary Adventure*," in the encounter with that old recluse, the Man of the Hill, who ambiguously combines features of two notable romance figures, the contemplative hermit and the embittered traveler.[20] And he rescues an afflicted "maiden"—"the reliefe of distressed women" being, as Lodge's Saladyne declares, "the speciall point, that Gentlemen are tied vnto by honour"[21]—although the outcome is regrettably rather too like Ruggiero's rescue of Angelica in *Orlando Furioso*, wherein the hero finds the naked body mounted behind him on his horse far too seductive to resist and, forgetting his proper love, decides to enjoy the rescued maiden himself.[22] The "Banquet of Sense" that follows in *Tom Jones* has epic-romance analogues enough; and the consequent reversal of the pursuing action, as we have also observed, had been given significant thematic overtones by Boiardo and Ariosto.

In the ungracious world of London, defined by an ambience of modern comic-stage intrigue, "she-tragedies," and erotic-pathetic ladies' novels, the romance hero is confronted with the alien "reality-principle" of a world where the pressing need for money is not only actual but primary—for "that Position of some Writers of Romance, that a Man can live altogether on Love" (the emphasis of the love-focused salon romances) the narrator supposes to be not altogether true (13.6), and Jones must borrow a shilling for chair-hire from Partridge in order to go to the Masquerade. If the London scenes are not entirely grim—for we have here to do with a comic romance—they are, in accordance with Fielding's overall structural plan and central plot, a sober enough descent from the warmer, richer romance environments, in which "character" could appear less formulaic and domesticated. The London scenes conclude in that emblem of the city itself, the prison (or, as the fact is, the Gatehouse), which serves structurally for the hero as a Janus-gate. It is the natural conclusion of his path through the City of Destruction, where Tom's own culpable submission to the vagaries of Fortune is reinforced by the treachery and malice of those about him; but it is also the setting in which the hero's regeneration and achievement of his freedom from Fortune's sway is celebrated, and the path out can only lead upward.

As Jones, after his release and recognition, prepares for the crucial meeting with a still angry Sophia, Partridge helps him to dress and recalls all the omens and presages and dreams that had prefigured a happy outcome. But the erring Mr. Jones is less certain of his reception: as Pyrocles in the *Arcadia* begs forgiveness of his mistress Philoclea and is told, "the punishment I desire of you shalbe your own conscience," so when Tom asks if he is never to hope for forgiveness, Sophia replies, "I think, Mr. *Jones* ... I may almost depend on your own Justice, and leave it to yourself to pass Sentence on your own Conduct." "Alas! Madam," answers Jones, "it is Mercy, and not Justice, which I implore at your Hands" (18.12). If Sophia, as has long been recognized, has the mythopoeic role as well as the name of Wisdom, she is wisdom at a less exalted level than the Divine Wisdom imaged forth by Beatrice in the *Commedia*. Sophia represents the essence of that social wisdom of which Woman had normally in the romances been the conserver and cherisher; and her beauty and desirability are inextricably joined with her intuitive sense of the social norms—she will not wed a confirmed libertine. Her rebuke (in this, at least, like that of Beatrice to Dante) invites and marks the transition to a profounder love. Sophia, as she herself declares, has not the high wisdom required to assess Jones's passionate declaration of sincerity; and, like Chaucer's formel eagle, who also "wol nat serve Venus ne Cupide," she has only one sure test of sincerity: "Time, ... Time alone, Mr. *Jones*, can convince me that you are a true Penitent." She suggests perhaps "A Twelvemonth"; but the very setting of a date tells us that a submerged voice in Sophia is really crying, with Rosalind, "Come, woo me, woo me! for now I am in a holiday humour, and like enough to consent." Sophia's role as princess of love promises a forgiveness that her sterner role as the embodiment of social wisdom cannot so easily provide; and in the end, like Laudine in Chrétien's *Yvain*, urged by her lords to wed Yvain immediately, she "finally speaks to the same intent as she would have done, indeed, if every one had opposed her wish."[23] If Tom Jones as a character, youthful emblem of *potentia*, gains his full dimension from the great tradition that provides his proper ambience, so Sophia as the romance heroine is his richly realized completion and fulfillment, the complementary element that alone can define his mature *essentia*.

Space (and perhaps the reader's patience) cannot allow full documentation of the many archetypal romance figures who appear in *Tom Jones*:

Bridget Allworthy, the "maiden" scornful of suitors, who secretly bears the hero; Squire Western, the *senex iratus* and father of the princess; Partridge, the amiable, cowardly, confident Squire; the Evil Counselors, who so frequently in the romances force the hero's exile; Mrs. Honour, the *confidante*, who is (very) like Juliet's nurse in offering poor consolation when the hero is banished; even the abruptly introduced Mrs. Arabella Hunt, whose proffer of marriage echoes the critical and ultimate test of the hero's fidelity in many a romance; and the ubiquitous Dowling, the carrier of the secret. No character is too small to swell the romance pageant and to further the purposes of providence. As Sir Philip Sidney observes, when the clodpoll herdsman Dametas in the *Arcadia*, attempting to frustrate the plans of the lovers, actually ushers in the desirable dénouement:

> The almightie wisdome evermore delighting to shewe the world, that by unlikeliest meanes greatest matters may come to conclusion: that humane reason may be the more humbled, and more willinglie geve place to divine providence: as at the first it brought in *Damœtas* to play a part in this royall pageant, so having continued him still an actor, now that all things were growne ripe for an end, made his folly the instrument of revealing that, which far greater cunning had sought to conceale.[24]

One character should perhaps receive fuller comment, however; for he has been seldom understood and, indeed, is not to be "understood" except in terms of his role in a comic romance, for as with all the other figures this *is* his essential literary character and he does not possess an extra-literary scientific "psychology." Mr. Allworthy's all-worthiness has been a constant issue in commentaries upon *Tom Jones*, and little reptile critics have not scrupled confidently to declare that a great artist did not know what he was doing when he created the good squire. Aside from the hubris involved in such an assumption, it is quite apparent that Fielding knew very well what he was doing, within the conventions of romance. Allworthy's "character" is part of the given, the *donnée*, in a romance (like the "fairy-tale" opening of *King Lear*, so natural in Shakespeare's romance context, so distressing to "realistic" criticism), and the long previous history of his role as *senex* and as *sapiens* and as the Deceived King of romance makes him the embodiment of a perfectly familiar complex of assumptions—which also, however, symbolized a continual and ever-during perplexity. For, from the point of view of the young, all "authority," even the most benevolent and loved, must be to some degree irrational, tyrannical, marked by a failure in understanding. This has ever been so, and myth and legend (and romance) have always intuitively grasped the fact. Allworthy's actions are seen in such a light through the perspective of young Tom Jones, since Jones is the focus of the narrative; but these same actions are simultaneously and quite differently assessed by the mature narrator. This highly complex dual vision—achieved as well with various other characters—in the case of Allworthy authentically renders with equal force both the pitiless judgment of youth upon its uncomprehending mentors and the certain assurance of age and experience that it possesses hard-won truth; and in his benevolent, just, and mistaken *senex*-figure Fielding preserves for us the inherent ambiguities that will always lie in parental power, indeed in power of any nature.

Allworthy is also, very significantly in a romance frame, "the Deceived King," whose most obvious archetype is the great emperor Charlemagne, bluntly displayed as Ganelon's dupe in the chronicle of Pseudo-Turpin, as he had been to an extent even in the *Chanson de Roland*. As his "historical" character was humanized in the romances that focused upon Roland (Orlando), Charlemagne or Carlo Magno became more and more assimilated to the wrathful father of ancient myth and folklore, easily practised upon by villainous deceivers—although it must be noted as of fundamental consequence for later fiction that he never lost in these narratives the dignity and honor and respect due his high office. This ambivalent balance is maintained in Pulci and Boiardo and Ariosto, as it had been even in the popular old tale of *Huon of Bordeaux*, where Charlemagne believes the lies of the evil brother Girard and, after a trial, condemns the innocent Huon—but is, nevertheless, insistently declared by the narrator to be a totally worthy monarch, a man of goodness and moderation. The like is true of such later Charlemagne-figures as King Lisuarte in *Amadis de Gaule* (who must in addition carry the burden of playing the tyrannical father of the princess, like old Capulet or his lineal descendant Squire Western); for, although Lisuarte listens to evil counselors and banishes Amadis from his service, the entire blame falls upon the counselors, not upon the "wise, vertuous and temperate" king himself. The traditional discrimination, fully realized in Fielding's erring but wise Allworthy, is compendiously exhibited in the words of Leonidas, hero of the "romance" plot of Dryden's *Marriage à la Mode*:

> First scorn'd, and now commanded from the Court!
> The King is good; but he is wrought to this
> By proud *Argaleon's* malice....[25]

Throughout the whole rich tradition we never once find any interest in the "psychology" of the Deceived King. What we do find is a profound and illuminating and perhaps disturbing commentary upon the nature of "goodness" and the ambiguities of maturity and power.

CHAPTER 5

# *Ethos* / The Dimension of Meaning

Plainly, Theme or "Meaning" can appear in (or be abstracted from) a work of art in a number of different ways.[1] It may even be stated directly, and in this case our modern term to express the distaste we feel for such a palpable design upon us—whether in Sidney or D. H. Lawrence—is "didactic." The reader who seeks to enjoy romance, however, must make at least a minimal effort to overcome this modern aversion; for, although there are degrees of palpability, the romances are for the most part either explicitly or implicitly and allegorically didactic, and their authors (and critics) would have found works that failed in didacticism as an ultimate end to be mere trivial entertainments. On the other hand, as modern criticism has been more apt to see than nineteenth-century middle-class commentary on fiction, "meaning" does not depend entirely upon overt declaration: it is inherent in the significant structure of a work of art, in the acts of its characters, in the uses of setting, and, centrally, in the style and language-choices and point-of-view of the writer. Such implicit meanings may not, as our more extravagant seekers after "latent" and "depth" structures believe, altogether take precedence over explicit levels of meaning; but they are important, they do signify.

The romance, once again like classic comedy, normally finds its very *raison d'être*—and, at the least, its rationale—in the illustration, demonstration, or celebration of a body of presumed and *à priori* truths, an emotionally charged as well as sense-making set of principles about the nature of the cosmos and of man. Its heroes search, in Stanley Fish's phrase, for values that have already found them. This is quite as true of a pagan work such as the *Metamorphoses* of Apuleius or the *Aethiopian History* of Heliodorus as it is of the romances of Chrétien de Troyes or the *Arcadia* of Sir Philip Sidney.

As I have earlier suggested, the dependence of all elements of the romance narrative upon the assumption of a rational cosmos—in the face of all the obvious irrationality of man's own habitation—makes for an inherently integrated work of art, despite the great variety of local scenes and actions, because all the elements work toward a common demonstration and derive from a common structural premise. The fact that this premise is dualistic or multi-leveled in nature, however, means that various parts of the narrative will contribute toward the common endeavor in different ways—much as any hierarchical social structure was presumed to function. The often episodic, disconnected, arbitrary successions of events, like the often irrational or unexpected acts or decisions of the characters, testify to ("mean") a level of the universe in which Fortune and the dominance of mere sense-experience and the corruption of sin join in the creation of apparent chaos. What the totality of the narrative celebrates, however, is the fact that, transcending this very human realm and interacting with it through the spiritual link of man's soul and the ever-accessible grace of God, is a paradigmatic level of the universe in which Providence and intellectual and moral certainty reign —in a word, the *intelligible* universe. This two-fold assumption is the thematic heart of the romance tradition; and it informs all the acts of the characters as well as all the narrative strategies.

More particular and immediately arresting themes are also, of course, the concern of particular narratives—dramatizations of all the Seven Mortal Sins as well as of the infinitude of human follies, celebrations of the fundamental needs and desires of the human soul, and renewings of the ritual-actions that epitomize the universal patterns of human existence. Since the "real" is conceived to lie in a dimension beyond the "actual"—the masquerade world of mere appearances—ultimate significance derives from the assessment of human actions in a larger, more inclusive perspective than "actuality" affords. Hence "meaning" in the romance is often symbolic, typological, emblematic, even allegorical. It is not a meaning derived from induction of particulars, nor is it "emergent" from the action; it is deductive and *à priori*, based on cultural norms (although this clearly does not mean that there are no conflicting ideas or themes). And since these cultural norms remained, all things considered, remarkably consistent through the varying generations of hierarchical societies resting upon an agricultural foundation, the "meanings" and ethical concerns of the great variety of romances over two thousand years also remain remarkably of a piece in their fundamental assumptions. This, incidentally, is also why Cicero, as a moralist, could seem to Henry Fielding almost a contemporary.

\* \* \*

Thematically, *Tom Jones* is, like the traditional romances, the demonstration and celebration of a universal, generic body of truths that are assumed *à priori*, rather than the induction of a personal and individual truth that is "emergent" from a world of undifferentiated particulars. (And, moral relativism or not, Western culture continues to share many "à priori" convictions, a truism amusingly exploited in the title of Malcolm Bradbury's play some years back, *Eating People Is Wrong*.) Nevertheless, as with the romances, the particular action of *Tom Jones* will take place in the world of the "actual"; and it is as the moral norms, the regulative conceptions, are tested and examined in a score of changing situations, and are manipulated and arranged in thoughtful patterns, that we are brought to understand their rational complexity and to feel their ultimate validity. This was, of course, the traditional rationale of fiction, as of rhetoric, and few were the defenders of the art of narrative who did not point out that Christ himself had chosen for that very reason to teach through fictions, by parables.

The ultimate and overarching theme of Fielding's comic romance is that the world makes sense: "Tho' Man's a fool, yet God is wise." I shall have to speak (again) of the providential universe that the very structure of Fielding's work demonstrates and celebrates; but there are less cosmic themes that play an important role in his narrative and I shall first consider a few (only) of these more immediate, though never more important, concerns. Fielding's dedication to *Tom Jones* declares that his theme is Goodness and Innocence. This is assuredly true, but it represents a somewhat more complex topic than the words may suggest to modern ears. By "innocence" he meant the condition of youth as it enters upon the inevitable process of testing out and probing the official values of its culture, the precondition of maturity in any effective society; by "goodness" he meant quite obviously more than the "goody-goodness" urged for youth by a postromantic ethos—what he meant was the acceptance of the conditions of human existence without malice, a very profound and (for the "Modern" liberal consciousness) a very startling proposition.

Fielding's structural pattern of Exile, Initiation, and Return echoed perhaps the most ancient and pervasive of mythical paradigms precisely because he was dramatizing one of the most ancient (and modern) of human themes, the coming of age. Although his tradition was less interested in developmental "process" than in the qualitative stages of human growth, and did not accept the language of determinism, a statement in terms of modern scientific gradualism is here not altogether inapposite. The "gradual unfolding of power and capacity," says a distinguished modern sociologist, is "a universal, biologically conditioned, and inescapable fact":

> This personal transition, or temporal progress, or change, may become closely linked with what may be called cosmic and societal time. The attempt to find some meaning in personal temporal transition may often lead to identification with the rhythms of nature or history, with the cycles of the seasons, with the unfolding of some cosmic plan (whether cyclical, seasonal, or apocalyptic), or with the destiny and development of society. The nature of this linkage often constitutes the focus round which an individual's personal identity becomes defined in cultural terms and through which personal experience, with its anguish, may be given some meaning in terms of cultural symbols and values.[2]

The youthful search for meaning and value becomes a type of adult mankind's own continuing search, as youth's often fumbling quest is a type of the failures and confusions that mark any honest pursuit of truth—or of full maturity. Fielding did indeed link Tom's quest with the rhythms of nature and the cycles of the seasons,[3] as Tom's circular path and ultimate achievement also provided a structural analogue for what the plot dramatizes, the eternal round of generation succeeding generation. Tom Jones's personal anguish and his youthful joys are "actual" enough in themselves; but it is Fielding's task to place them in a social and intellectual and cosmic context that makes them more acutely "real" and meaningful.

The social context is strongly shaped by Fielding's comic vision. We are told by modern sociology that "deception and self-deception" are at the very heart of social reality, that a society can maintain itself "only if its fictions (its 'as if' character, to use Hans Vaihinger's term) are accorded ontological status by at least some of its members some of the time."[4] Not to enter into the many dilemmas of "bad faith" and the like that this argument poses, we may at least see that comedy is then highly "subversive" in one sense, for its natural tendency is to expose the reigning social fictions *as* fictions (satire, of course, may do this even more brutally); but, like the Gorgon's blood, if it can destroy, it can also heal—for the conclusion of a comedy almost inevitably reinstates the necessary fictions as ontological reality, modified or qualified perhaps, but "real." The "happy ending" of comedy—and of the comic romance—is thus a happy ending in two senses (or more), for besides bringing its tale to a fortunate conclusion suggestive of reintegration and renewal and the ultimate providential *telos*, it also validates the superior ontological dimension or component of the socially "actual," after having employed the license of comedy—its "laboratory" of alternative fictions and possibilities—to expose the deception and self-deception of existent values. This is what C. L. Barber has called "the clarification about limits which comes from going beyond the limit."[5]

And it is in "the clarification about limits"—the limits of such a virtue as Prudence, which can poison itself with the antidote, the limits of engaging animal vitality, the limits of desirable social protocol, the limits of merely human justice (or merely human mercy), the limits of language itself,[6] and the limits of innocence and experience—that Fielding's deep and resonant classical wisdom is most typically exhibited. He understands very well the "borderline" situations in human morality: but, as with any mature artist, his pull is always toward the norm, toward the recognition of limit. Not, however, without a full appreciation of the ambiguities of the norm itself. Romance literature, like Angus Fletcher's "Allegory," very much tends to display towards its polar antagonisms a certain ambivalence: "The heart of moralizing actions becomes temptation, which asserts the desirability of evil (a paradox inherent in the very idea of absolute moral standards)."[7] The function of comic romance, one may say, is to allow us to experience the desirability of evil without encouraging us to succumb to it, something that romance authors like Spenser and Milton (for instance) thoroughly understood.

That Henry Fielding is a Christian author, working imaginatively and individually within a highly traditional set of assumptions has become a matter of general comprehension among the literate in recent years, and his personal leaning toward the so-called "Latitudinarian" interpretation of Christian dogma has been well documented. There is, however, a more inclusive sense in which Fielding's world of moral value transcends any historical orthodoxy, not only because it is profoundly "classical" as well as specifically Christian, but because it is ultimately rooted in a full and generous experiential awareness of human frailty and human possibility that is more comprehensive than the formal interpretation of experience offered by a particular dogma will ordinarily encompass. Despite the vivifying certainties of his faith in a providential cosmos, there is always at the level of mere human "actuality," a tentativeness of judgment, an openness to fresh experience, in Fielding's moral world, which is perhaps what he meant to convey when he said, "I am not writing a System, but a History . . ." (12.8).

Fielding's "morality" is, of course, by no means merely the ethics of "the good heart" (I do not suppose that any but critics who get their background material from undergraduate outline-guides need to be told this, but one still hears it from such persons); nor does he believe in the "natural goodness" of all mankind—the full articulation of that absurd doctrine is a later development. He had himself shaped at least one play (*The Good-Natured Man*) and several comic romances to suggest that purely "spontaneous" emotive virtues offered an inadequate measure of full moral being and maturity. Nevertheless, he did believe that there is in some (perhaps many) human beings a latent capacity for loving behavior, a "natural Goodness of Heart," that it was the crucial function of the responsible moralist to nurture and encourage. Since the mass of mankind is, however, inevitably and always busily involved in its own self-seeking and self-justifying enterprises of *mauvaise foi*, mere "good-nature" has not only its own very considerable flaws to regard, but has a difficult path to tread in the world of the "actual." As St. Augustine somewhere observes, it is one thing to love man, another to put your trust *in* man. This is, of course, the compelling reason for the centrality of *prudentia* in Fielding's moral universe: with his mentor Cicero he recognized that the man seeking to realize his potential humanity in a world well populated with the vicious and the crafty and the self-seeking (in a word, the creatures who follow an equally "natural" instinct) has compelling need to bring all his moral intelligence to bear upon his own weakness and the fact of human depravity.[8] It is a lesson that, as always, comes hard to the amiable and unfocused energy of such as young Tom Jones—and unfortunately a lesson that experience alone must always teach the thoughtless.

When Mr. Allworthy, in the role both of the classic *sapiens* of philosophy and the classic *senex* of comedy, assesses the character of his unruly charge, Tom Jones, "in wholesome counsel to his unstaid youth,"[9] he declares:

> I am convinced, my Child, that you have much Goodness, Generosity, and Honour in your Temper; if you will add Prudence and Religion to these, you must be happy: For the three former Qualities, I admit, make you worthy of Happiness, but they are the latter only which will put you in Possession of it. (5.7)

This wisdom of aged experience, presented by Polonius to a dutiful Laertes, sounds precisely as "conventional," flat, and irrelevant to the reader (at this point) as it does to Jones, the warm youth setting out upon a voyage of personal discovery too "real" and urgent for such baggage. Dutiful or not, each young Euphues who hears old Eubulus tell him "that the tender youth of a childe is lyke the temperinge of newe waxe apte to recieue any forme," surely replies in his heart, "The similytude you rehearse of the waxe, argueth your waxinge and melting brayne."[10] Of course Fielding knew this as well as anyone; and Tom's warm and unfeigned gratitude to his benefactor offers no warrant that he has even heard the sage advice of that excellent man. Nor, if heard, that it will be heeded: Jones's very next actions will be to get drunk and to retire into the bushes with Molly Seagrim. Lyly offers a consolation—small, but a consolation—for the inevitable outcome of this anciently iterated scene: "It hath bene an olde sayed sawe, and not of lesse truth then antiquitie, that witte is the better if it bee the deerer bought: as in the sequele of thys historie shall moste manifestly appeare."[11] Tom Jones, too, will buy his wisdom more dearly than at the bedside of his foster-father.

Fielding surely believes in the fresh, rejuvenating impulse of youth; but he does not believe with popular romanticism that this is all there is to human life. Mere innocence, mere "spontaneity," the mere "good heart" will prove in his narrative to be often of positive value, but also quite unequal to the complexities of mature moral experience in the world of the "actual"; and, indeed, will prove to be not without failings inherent in the good heart's outgoing and unthinking emotional valences toward others. For these can be not only mindlessly indiscriminate but also can consider the illumined object of such a valence as a thing, not a person. This, as Fielding more than once points out to us, is mere *amor ferinus*, a self-serving lust that loses all sense of the humanity, the "person-ness" of its object.

Perhaps only comedy, among literary forms, has the capacity to do full justice to the ambivalencies and absurdities of this eternal moral dilemma—and particularly to that aspect of it which has to do with the sexual behavior of human beings. Two of Fielding's predecessors in Christian romance *comoedia*—Dante and Chaucer—are sterner moralists than he; but he is at one with them in neither giving sanction to sexual license nor supposing it to be the most weighty of human sins. As Dante's circles of Hell and Purgatory and Chaucer's *Parson's Tale* very sharply remind us, and as romance and comedy have always tried to remind us, the sins of pride and hypocrisy and self-love and envy and malice and treachery are of far greater magnitude and are a far more certain index to the moral status of any human being than that least of sins (if none the less inescapably a sin), *luxuria*, lechery. The middle-class nineteenth century would make of sexual behavior the prime measure of moral character: but the genuinely obscene resides in the lower circles of Hell. This is the prevailing moral view of all the traditional romances, including the "chivalric": only the effeminate neoplatonizing salon romances of the seventeenth century elevated an obsession with proud and self-serving chastity and with the minute punctilios of sexual "decency" to a truly central place in their moral universe. Unfortunately, it was precisely these romances, of which Fielding never ceased to make rational fun, that would shape the nineteenth-century bourgeois-effeminate notion of "romance" and provide modern literary historians with their misconceptions about the entire romance tradition.

The ruling theme of romance discourse on sex is neither chastity nor license but the eternal, universal, and very complicated matter of somehow bringing a necessary and inevitable biological drive within the frame of an equally necessary social and spiritual continuity. Or, as usually conceived, incorporating the natural urge of sexuality within the sacramental (in the general, as well as the specifically Catholic, sense) and social frame of Marriage.

> O heaven and earth (said *Musidorus*) to what a passe are our mindes brought, that from the right line of vertue, are wryed to these crooked shifts? But ô Love, it is thou that doost it: thou changest name upõ name; thou disguisest our bodies, and disfigurest our mindes. But in deed thou hast reason, for though the wayes be foule, the journeys end is most faire and honourable.[12]

In an older sacramental frame, as we may perhaps forget, an actual realignment of the *soul* had been presumed to occur through the sacrament of marriage: the passions were brought within the proper dominion of reason, of moral wisdom (*sophia*), and the will was transformed by the redirection of the lustful impulse to its proper and desirable ends. This ancient "psychology" was not outmoded by the technical reconsideration of the Sacraments that marked the Reformation.

The "foule wayes" to this "faire and honourable" journey's end lie through the realm of Fortune; and the course of true love seldom does run smooth in the romances. Tom and Sophia may echo the cry of Shakespeare's Proteus, "O, that our fathers would applaud our loves, / To seal our happiness with their consents!"—but there are always blocking elements, and not only for narrative reasons. As Prospero, manager of the scene of youthful love, observes:

> They are both in either's powers; but this swift business
> I must uneasy make, lest too light winning
> Make the prize light....[13]

The distinction between fidelity and lightness in human love perhaps echoes at a distance the profounder distinction between sacred and profane love. But these are not Victorian distinctions: that *beau idéal* of the Renaissance, Amadis de Gaule, consummates his love with Oriana in the first book of the narrative, although they are quite unmarried, and she bears a child secretly; but Amadis is no light lover—he remains throughout all difficulties and temptations the very type of the totally faithful lover. His brother, Galaor, on the other hand, wanders light-heartedly and uncommittedly through the tale collecting trophies of love; and—like Tom Jones—he is as often the seduced as the seducer. Rescued damosels—like Mrs. Waters—prove appropriately grateful in *Amadis de Gaule*, and as the translator puts it, after one rescue: "During these speeches, Galaor still held his loue in his armes, kissing and toying with her so pleasantly, as *Diana* soone after lost her interest in the maiden...."[14]

Tom Jones is converted to an Amadis, a truly faithful lover, before the conclusion of the narrative; but in his inherent and indiscriminate gallantry of nature, he is the Galaor-figure. Except that *he* will suffer for it, particularly in his degrading liaison with autumnal Lady Bellaston. The narrative perspective of benign maturity in comedy and romance had traditionally regarded youthful sexuality with the tolerance that saw it as a transient phase, the "decorum" (in its rightful sense) of Youth's role: "Our own precedent passions do instruct us / What levity's in youth ..."; and life as well as literature supported Fielding's declaration that "Young Men of open, generous Dispositions are naturally inclined to Gallantry" (4.5). A long array of romance heroes had succumbed to the urgent temptation; and one, Sir Degaré, was even rather sharply twitted for falling asleep in a magic castle, rather than enjoying the maidens at his disposal there; for, as Ariosto's Ricciardetto put it, to refuse a desirous lady was scarcely befitting a warrior.[15] Nevertheless, behind all these instances normally lay an ironic reservation: the true Christian hero *should* have the spiritual strength to resist that temptation to behave like a merely sensate creature bereft of a rational soul. And throughout his own comic romance, Fielding in this highly ambiguous matter was able to draw upon a body of lore, traditional romance situations, that ironically "supported" one kind of value (the sensual and the "vital"), which would in the sequel be unequivocally brought into question. For, in the romance view—and in Fielding's—what is *merely* "vital" may be also merely animal. We see in young Tom Jones all those potentialities both for good and evil that, in a more sublime but not less traditional or serious context, Beatrice had remarked in Dante, endowed potentially with graces that should have brought "a wondrous harvest":

> But so much ranker, weedier, and more gross
> Runs the untended field where wild tares seed,
> As the good soil is rich and vigorous.
> .........................................
> And by wild ways he wandered, seeking for
> False phantoms of the good, which promise make
> Of joy, but never fully pay the score.[16]

Tom Jones will have to wander by a number of wild ways before the truth of this ancient wisdom, precisely describing his situation, will even vaguely begin to dawn upon him. But his creator has known it all along.

His literary creator must also judge Tom. The "popular" understanding of *Tom Jones* has seldom comprehended this, naively imagining that because Fielding *shows* Jones "skylarking," he therefore entirely endorsed that behavior. Clearly he did not, and Tom will pay for his insouciance. What Fielding did endorse, however, as comedy forever has, even in the most spiritual or skeptical contexts, was the life-affirming outgoingness that lay behind the comical indiscriminateness of youthful passion. He distinguished traditionally enough between mere casual lust ("the Desire of satisfying a voracious Appetite with a certain Quantity of delicate white human Flesh") and genuine love, " which is gratified by contributing to the Happiness of others"; but he was too perceptive not to recognize "that this Love when it operates towards one of a different Sex, is very apt, towards its complete Gratification, to call in the Aid of that Hunger which I have mentioned above" (6.1)[17] So that, if Tom's vigorous appetites too easily master him (and judgment will be passed on this), those very appetites are nevertheless testimony to the *potentia*, "the good soil," that will issue in an essential maturity of health, normality, and high capacity for love. Fielding calls upon all the resources of his rich and flexible style to maintain both sides of this timeless paradox, to keep alive the reader's sympathy for his young and vital hero without for a moment sanctioning his wayward behavior or those moral lapses, "which, as is the Nature of Vice, brought sufficient Punishment upon him themselves" (11.10).

This is a more difficult artistic (and moral) task than one may at first appreciate. Silenus and Priapus hover about the comic scene; for, whether or not Aristotle's historical derivation was accurate, classic comedy—the tradition behind the comic romance—is in its essence a phallic song, a celebration of fertility and life. But, since it is also in its essence a *social* mode, it is inevitably concerned with limits and with judgment. The fundamental confrontation of comedy, between the Fathers and the Sons, the claims of Law and the claims of Liberty, must somehow be mediated; and this is an artistic (and moral) demand to which surprisingly few writers have been equal. To flout the Law is both easy and gratifying—it is the immature romantic version of "Liberty." But to offer a holiday from legalism while firmly asserting the ultimate rightness of the Law is something that only the most mature artists have been able to encompass.

Fielding's success in this difficult endeavor comes, in part, as a gift of the comic tradition. The basic plot of Roman comedy offers a resolution in which, although the Sons have triumphed over the Fathers, liberty over law, the affirmation of "life" over the constrictions of age, the Sons are nevertheless brought once again within the social frame—with all its fundamental claims upon them. The marriage of Tom and Sophia, of undirected vitality and social wisdom ("Madam," says Amadis to Oriana, "your discretion hath surmounted my folly")[18] offers the traditional emblematic guarantee that the loving, thoughtless youth, who has challenged and tested in his own individual way the bounds of his society's norms, has been reintegrated within that society, and that in the never-ending, never-changing conflict between the claims of Liberty and the claims of Law a new accommodation and a fresh beginning have been made. For society is a new thing, the Law itself is a new thing, with each progressive reincorporation of its rebels.

But if Roman comedy gave Fielding this essential resolution, the warm, humane, and rational ethos of *Tom Jones* is very individually his own. As a thoughtful student of social behavior, as well as a professional student of the law, he understood in their most profound dimensions the paradoxes of morality and freedom. Christian apologists for fiction, as I have remarked, were pleased to argue that Christ taught by "fictions": and it may well be that, when one confronts the opposing but complementary demands of Liberty and of Law, or of Love and of Justice, that the first terms of these oppositions can most effectively be conveyed by fictions, the latter terms in discursive prose. In his essays, Fielding tended to stress the claims of society and of the law; in his fictions, the claims of the individual and of love; but in neither mode did he ignore or deny the valid contrary claims. In *Tom Jones*, the amateur highwayman is allowed by Tom to go free, despite Partridge's protestations, and this humane act is validated by the narrative. After seeing the man's regeneration, Tom later reflects with horror "on the dreadful Consequences which must have attended [his family], had he listened rather to the Voice of strict Justice, than to that of Mercy when he was attacked on the high Road" (13.10). However, the argument of "those of a more saturnine Temper," expressed vigorously by Partridge, would see Tom's act as "a Want of Regard to that Justice which every Man owes his Country" (12.14); and, however poor the instrument of this claim in *Tom Jones*, this would be precisely the burden of Fielding's own earnest comment upon the public's duty to give evidence and to forward prosecutions, in the *Enquiry into the Causes of the Late Increase of Robbers* (1751). Thus the general "legalistic" principle that robbers should be prosecuted for the good of society is not *negated* by the presentation in *Tom Jones* of the fictive affirmation, in a particular case of conscience, that mercy may sometimes represent the higher justice.

The "legalistic" element in religion and philosophy is, of course, essentially negative, a set of prohibitions—or, where it is positive, tends to propose an ideal of the truly "real" well beyond human achieving. Fielding accepted *both* the legalistic and the idealistic imperatives as necessary and desirable controls in the moral life of a healthy society: but he also recognized that the noble self-transcending ideals of Christianity or of (say) Stoicism or of the magnificent structure of the Law, required a balancing element that alone could enable them to function in any truly effective way in the world of the "actual." Divine justice and divine mercy, Fielding knew, provided the ultimate model and the ultimate sanction for merely human law: but, as imperfect human Justice must constantly be corrected and qualified by reference to that ideal, so must it be balanced by (however imperfect) human Mercy, and so must the formal majesty of the law be balanced by some mode of equity or moral casuistry that will adjust and temper necessary forms to particular cases. Both Fielding's temper and his training, as well as the literary traditions he chose to follow, made this needful moral, social, legal equipoise a central imperative of his art. It was essentially a balance of opposing goods (the Western tradition had not yet "evolved" to the immature cant of defining both society and law as inherently evil); and Fielding's narrative, indeed his very style, down to its smallest elements, maintained that vivifying balance—where, as Professor Gombrich says of Keats's *Urn*, a plentitude of values is held in miraculous equilibrium.[19]

The rejection of Blifil by Allworthy, a *scène à faire* in comic romance—the casting out of the *pharmakos*, the separation of the emblematic figure of self-serving evil from the newly crystallized community—is a scene conducted with sensitive respect for the logic of the narrative, what the reader has been brought to desire, but also with a discriminating sense, even in such a "polar" situation, of the competing claims of justice and mercy. "And now a Message was brought from Mr. *Blifil*, desiring to know if his Uncle was at Leisure, and he might wait upon him. *Allworthy* started and turned pale, and then in a more passionate Tone than, I believe, he had ever used before, bid the Servant tell *Blifil*, he knew him not" (18.11). This is the stern justice that places beyond the pale a Lucio, a Shylock, a Don John ("Think not on him till to-morrow. I'll devise thee brave punishments for him. Strike up, pipers").[20] But there is another, more expansive, comic vision, that of Cymbeline: "Pardon's the word to all"; and it is for this that Jones, the man who has known the sting of injustice, speaks: "Consider, my dear Uncle, I was not myself condemned unheard." Blifil, now quite as servile and mean as he had before been wicked and arrogant (and shedding tears that flow not from contrition but as "the Effects of that Concern which the most savage Natures are seldom deficient in feeling for themselves"), welcomes Jones's forgiveness and offer of money, and then departs the house. Mercy has been fictively argued, even for the least deserving and most inhuman: but Justice has been achieved. In the case of Black George Seagrim, however, Allworthy remains inflexible despite Tom's plea: "Such mistaken Mercy is not only Weakness, but borders on Injustice ..." (18.11).

> Mercy is not itself, that oft looks so;
> Pardon is still the nurse of second woe.[21]

Fielding had more than once argued, in a traditional classical-Christian vein, that mere indiscriminate charity (the untutored "good heart") could very well prove destructive of a genuine and effective charity; so too could he feel the force of an Allworthy's argument on indiscriminate mercy. But if, in the formal and professional argument of the *Enquiry into the Causes of the Late Increase of Robbers*, "the Passions of the Man are to give Way to the Principles of the Magistrate," in his comic romance we have a forum in which the entitlements of both man and magistrate are fictively embodied and balanced. As *sapiens* and as *senex*, Allworthy is representative of a justice that is stern and even sometimes mistaken but that is nevertheless, in Fielding's portrait, honorable and equable; as *adulescens*, Tom presents the warm-hearted but undiscriminating case for an all-forgiving mercy. If neither can be said to "triumph" in their continuing confrontation, as neither decisively can in human society, there is yet no doubt for the reader that the narrative sanction falls on the side of forgivenes and of love. For that is the ultimate promise of Fielding's providential world itself.

Even if we did not know that Fielding personally and profoundly believed in an existent Providence, transcending the realm of fortune and of folly, we might expect to find it in his history as a literary given. For, as I have declared, the tradition in which he worked would have made the providential frame almost inescapable for his fictive universe. Not only has comedy from its very beginnings offered a secular analogue for a world of providential order and benevolent design, but the tradition of romance has equally insisted upon such a necessary level of eternal, universal Being, beyond the flux of mere Becoming—as a handful of instances (from hundreds) may compendiously suggest. Apuleius concludes the *Metamorphoses* with fortune-driven Lucius's discovery that Isis has overseen (and alone can rescue him from) his futile efforts to master human disorder through secular magic; and Heliodorus in the *Aethiopian History* constantly insists upon the operation of providence in a world of apparently chaotic chance meetings and accidents of fortune. Such pagan schemata were, of course, accommodated with ease to the aims of Christian romance, in which the very fact of contingency and chance was itself an aspect of providence; and the medieval romances, never *merely* "secular," make the dramatic interplay between an almost reified *Fortuna* and an overruling and inclusive Providence central to their thematic purposes, as to their structures. This cosmic scheme equally informs the romance-epics and romances of the Renaissance: even Ariosto, who typically directs his characters in the world of the "actual" by Fortune, does not fail to characterize it (anglicized by Harington) as the mere "Fortune that helps frantike men and drunke";[22] and Sidney's *Arcadia*, which with equal frequency insists upon the metaphor of Fortune, concludes with the firm declaration that "all had fallen out by the highest providence."[23] There is no need, one may suppose, for citations from such obvious attestors as Spenser and Milton and Bunyan; but it may at first sight appear startling to the uninitiated to find that even William Congreve orders his *Incognita* in the same familiar terms.[24] Hence the image of a providential universe, in which the short-sighted and the careless fall under the (self-invoked) hand of mutable Fortune, can be seen as one that Fielding inherited with his romance structure and that he elaborated in terms of his own plot requirements and his own doctrinal leanings—and that he infused with his own genius—but that offered him, as it had his predecessors in romance, a rich and generous matrix of narrative possibilities and a formal structure that guaranteed to the apparently random and contingent actions of men a moral and thematic significance grander and more permanent than themselves.

CHAPTER 6

# *Logos* / Questions of Style

The romance tradition employed modes and levels of stylistic emphasis that ranged from the courtly artificiality (when "artificial" was a term of highest praise) of John Lyly's *Euphues* to the single-minded narrative drive of *King Horn*. Few romances sought after what would later be called by middle-class critics "the Sublime" (as in the claptrap mélange of Macpherson's *Ossian*);[1] but many of them did, like Chrétien de Troyes, seek some heightening beyond even the courtly language of their normal sponsors. The translation of Heliodorus offered the Renaissance a popular stylistic model; and, though not all romances affected the patterned prose of Lyly or Sir Philip Sidney, there was a general consciousness of the potency of unordinary language in narrative. The notable Renaissance absorption in a creative rhetoric, for instance, produced set discourses or "orations" (such as Mercutio's "Queen Mab" speech in *Romeo and Juliet* or the formal debates in Sidney's *Arcadia*) that the author often made a point of calling to the special attention of his audience, as among the most valid and pleasing elements of his literary art.

Even the protestation that one used no rhetoric was itself one of the conventions of classical rhetoric; and Saladyne's very highly wrought address to Aliena, in Lodge's *Rosalynde*, begins, "Faire Mistres, if I bee blunt in discouering my affections, and vse little eloquence in leuelling out my loues. ..."[2] Or, to move beyond England, there is perhaps no more transparent fictive "pretense" in literature than the courtly Ariosto's apology, "ben che col rozzo stil duro e mal atto...."[3] As one of the best modern readers of Shakespeare observes:

> The general Renaissance tendency frankly to accept and relish the artificiality of art, and the vogue of formal rhetoric and "conceited" love poetry, also made for sophistication about the artistic process. The sonneteers mock their mythological machinery only to insist the more on the reality of what it represents. ... Shakespeare's auditors had not been conditioned by a century and a half of effort to achieve sincerity by denying art.[4]

That is, they were neither "Romantic" *nor* "Realistic" in their attitude toward the fictive; and since this effectually exhausts the nineteenth-century critical postures, it should once again be obvious that a nineteenth-century critical vocabulary is incapable of dealing with the Romance—since it, too, is neither "Romantic" nor "Realistic." Moreover, in the essentially "oral" tradition of the romances, which asked that a story be *told* (or sung), the narrator was not asked to skulk somewhere behind his narrative, trembling lest he grow impure; his presence and his commentary, to be heard not "overheard," were taken for granted—there were merely competent and incompetent singers and tellers. As Bertrand Bronson declares, "Literature is so naturally, so fundamentally, an affair of *telling*, as opposed to *recording*, that the traces are omnipresent" in its whole history.[5]

It is true, on the other hand, that from the classic period a certain distrust of "mere" fictionality had existed (as it most potently still does). Since the "serious" popular romance was uncanonical in the classic world, it sought validation or perhaps respectability by claiming to be "history" and normally presented its tale on the "authority" of another. The comic romance, however, possibly granted the license of a unique vision that was inescapably fictive, seems to have felt no need to bow to such demands; and, as Ben Edwin Perry has noted, "all the comic romances known to us from antiquity are told in the person of the principal character speaking about his own experience," that is, they did not require the pretense that they were history, whose truth had to be formally vouched for by someone other than the author or the narrator himself.[6] Petronius and Apuleius and Lucian, although they employ the form and the type-characters found also in the "serious" romance based upon epic and historical-biographical models, exhibit a sophisticated impersonality toward the characters and their adventures and an intellectual concern that transcends and deepens the pure narrative entertainment. At a much later date, Cervantes is to be found mocking the "historical" claim of the peninsular romances by creating the absurd Cide Hamete Benengeli as *his* author (translated by a Moor) and thus insisting that his readers recognize the fictionality of fiction. Cervantes tells us at one point that Don Quixote is at Don Antonio's, "where we leave him for the present, because 'tis *Cid Hamet*'s Will and Pleasure it should be so."[7] This arbitrary proceeding signifies the author's control, not so much over the *events* of his tale, which are within the realm of the "actual" as that is defined by the initial conditions of the romance and the logic of the narrative, but rather over the *manner of relating* the tale, which is entirely within the author's prerogative. And it is in the exploitation of this stylistic prerogative that the full richness of the comic romance is most typically exhibited.

The principle of "decorum," or levels of language, that in one form or another reigned throughout the romance tradition,[8] reflected and complemented the hierarchical multi-leveled image of the cosmos and of human communal existence, providing the final link in the coherence and integral unity of the romance narrative. The possible variety of expressive modes thus inherently accessible to romance authors was perhaps not always exploited so fully as it might have been: but the possibilities were there. Language could run the gamut from an apparently "naive" openness to the most reticulated and enigmatic suggestiveness. The "matter" could be heightened, reduced, viewed ironically, celebrated, or whatever, as the "manner" of the narrator decreed, offering complexities of meaning and tone that can still gravel modern commentators. And to these complexities were added, in the comic romance, the even more sophisticated options of a calculated *indecorum*, which demanded of author and of audience the very highest perceptiveness and intellectual alertness.

\* \* \*

Except for mime, all dramatic and narrative art is dependent upon Language to achieve its ends; and a neutral or commonplace "transparent" style can offer only the ring-metal ere the ring be made. "Style" we may compendiously define as the aesthetic effect upon the capable reader (for the ass is deaf to the harp) of both conventional and idiosyncratic manipulations of language within a given contextual "world." Whether one conceives of style as significant "ornament," the dress of thought, in Renaissance terms, or as an integral process that through its own structures conveys "meaning," in modern monistic terms, Language is clearly central to the art of fiction. And, although Henry Fielding's theoretical position was that of Renaissance modal and tonal ornament ("the Cookery of the Author"), his practice exhibits most consummately the valid modern argument that the very structures of language themselves project meaning.

Fielding's high style is in the tradition of Heliodorus, of Chrétien, of *Amadis de Gaule*, Lyly, and Sidney, in its richness and fullness of range, its exploitation of rhetorical possibilities to express and subtly to modulate meaning, and in its formal grace; but before him, no author of prose fiction in English had so completely shaped this artful romance style into an instrument of flowing ease and simplicity as well as dignity. In great measure, the comic mode demanded such an "accommodation" of high art to ease of reception. The immediate function of language in comedy is to clarify and make perspicuous the lines of action and to establish unmistakably an atmosphere of warm good humor that conditions the reader to set aside whatever personal and ordinary expectations he may have about human experience for the more exhilarating and satisfying expectations of the comic vision of human possibility. Such a primary demand requires, of course, obvious and forcible cues to the special kind of "world" one is to enter (which is why even the most sophisticated comic dramatists from Aristophanes through Shakespeare unabashedly offer "low" horseplay in presenting their high comic vision); and in prose fiction these cues can most immediately and effectively be conveyed through the felt presence of the narrator—or what Wayne Booth has called the Implied Author, "not only to make us aware of the value system which gives it [the story] its meaning but, more important, to make us willing to accept that value system, at least temporarily."[9] Fielding, although he does declare (not altogether parodically) that his work is "history," in the mode of the "serious" romance, unquestionably accepts the fictionality of fiction, as the comic romances traditionally had, and suffers no trepidation at declaring himself flatly to be the Author as well as Narrator of *Tom Jones*, as he also insists upon his right to tell the story in his own way, so long as the conventions of a "private history," a fictional biography, are not violated.

The romance mode, that of the "serious" romance at least, usually maintained a fairly consistent style throughout, in which, indeed, the diction of the characters was often not notably different from that of the narrator—as Ben Jonson somewhat unjustly noted of the *Arcadia*, when he complained that "Sidney did not keep a Decorum in making every one speak as well as himself."[10] Comedy, or comic romance, on the other hand, although its style was expected to be low, *humilis*, was granted a variety of dictions, as Congreve reminded his readers with the famous line from Horace employed as epigraph to *The Double Dealer*: "interdum tamen et vocem Comoedia tollit."[11] Fielding, in joining comedy and romance made himself heir to a mixture of conventions that, as he could see in the instance of Cervantes, offered prose fiction the opportunity of being at once high art *and* an exploration of "ordinary" life. The basic romance mode was one of relative seriousness and dignity; and to this dimension Fielding's formal style—with its roots in the "loose Senecan" mode of such as Halifax and Temple, reshaped by Tillotson and Addison—was entirely faithful and unfailingly adequate.[12] But comedy by its very nature circles about the norms of the merely "serious" and through its armory of distorting lenses provides oblique perspectives upon those norms, as it also questions the set categories by which we presume to assess human experience. Its vision is not "assimilative," reducing all experience to one interpretation, but "open," free to express all the ambiguities not only of "actual" life but of that curious interaction between life and convention which we call art. Fielding could make evocative use of a number of existent individual genres (pastoral, epic, satire, even "tragedy"), as he could also exploit all the levels of style suggested by the theory of decorum, to create constantly shifting modes of viewing raw experience, which conclude in the illusion that life has been seen from every perspective open to man. It *is* an illusion, but it is a rich and liberating illusion.

Unlike any of the writers ordinarily considered as "novelists," with the possible exception of those other great mavericks, Laurence Sterne and James Joyce, Fielding was a master of the forms and modes of classical rhetoric. Since this mastery can be of small concern to the average critic of the Novel, it should be clear that an adequate appreciation of what Fielding has in fact achieved in *Tom Jones* cannot be arrived at *via* a critical vocabulary intended to explain or celebrate the "realistic" novel. His masterwork of narrative demands, rather, the modes of critical analysis involving a high consciousness of the arts of language that one would expect the historical critic to bring to the works of Ariosto or Sir Philip Sidney or Edmund Spenser or, most potently, William Shakespeare—who has also been trivialized by critics obsessed with "realism." All of these romance masters were also master rhetoricians and, as recent scholarship free of the old middle-class Romantic-Realist bias against classical rhetoric has capably demonstrated, the recovery of a rhetorical vocabulary enables us once again to appreciate their incredible achievement in something approaching its own terms and traditions.

I have elsewhere shown in some detail the fundamental role that classical rhetoric—the most highly developed model of language artistry—plays in *Tom Jones*; and I shall here simply repeat that "throughout *Tom Jones* characters argue, debate, advise, exhort, dissuade, praise, dispraise, and render judgments (even little sermons) on every subject and every course of action. And the Author of the whole lets his voice be heard as well, in all the forms of forensic, epideictic, and deliberative rhetoric."[13] It is as a master rhetorician that Fielding establishes that warm and fruitful bond between himself as Narrator and the hypothetical Reader which operates as a synecdoche for the relationship between his created "world" and the world of actual human experience and thought, the world of his audience.

In a sense, however, Fielding's major debt to the classical and romance tradition for a stylistic mastery almost unequalled in prose fiction may be found less in particular devices and techniques than in the ratification in its best examples of his conviction that prose fiction need not be a low and unliterary endeavor, a "romantick" or merely plausible gratification for contemporary unschooled readers with time on their hands, but that it could answer to the highest demands of the highest forms of art. Some few specifics of his particular stylistic debt may, however, be briefly noted in passing. The close relationship of the narrator to his audience, for instance, is scarcely Fielding's invention (although he made it among the most memorable in fiction); it is obviously enough a feature of the "oral" tradition in literature from the time of Homer. The numerous devices of anticipation ("as you shall learn hereafter," etc.) and reminder ("Heretofore it hath been declared, how *Amadis* being with *Briolania*, promised to reuenge the King her Fathers death...") are central elements of that oral tradition. The movement from one set of characters to another that occurs in almost all the major works of epic and romance sponsored formulas that were subject to high individualization: "Now leave we them kissing and clipping, as was kindly thing; and now speak we of Queen Guenever...." The narrator's ironic commentary upon his action was brought to a fine art in Ariosto; and the use of classical allusion and of extended simile to provide circles of implication for a given action was, from Chrétien on, a vital mode of heightening pleasure and value for the "neo-classical" narrative (meaning the entire Christian romance tradition). Even such devices as the alternative explanation, which Fielding makes into an instrument of calculated ambiguity, are as ancient as Homer (e.g., *Odyssey*, 7.261-63) and as "modern" as Tasso. The topos of Needless to Describe ("Yf blanchardyn was right glad of this aduenture / It is not to be axed"), related to that of Inability to Describe, was a rhetorical convention that clearly depended upon an audience of sufficient maturity and experience to "fill in" the passed-over matter; and both conventions had a long life: "and to tell the joys that were betwixt La Beale Isoud and Sir Tristram, there is no tongue can tell it, nor heart think it, nor pen write it."

All of these fine communal narrative devices were a gracious heritage from tradition: the unfailing rightness of Fielding's word-magic, however, is his achievement and his alone. One need not today argue at great length that "style" is inseparable from the other elements which interweave to produce a major work of art; but I should like to comment further (if inadequately for my subject) upon the integral role played by Fielding's narrative style as it contributes to the fullest realization of those particular elements that his critic has chosen to abstract: structure, setting, character, and theme.

The world that he created was, as I have observed, highly structured despite the apparent randomness of its foreground (actually not random at all, of course). In the levels of stylistic decorum, in the various rhetorical strategies, in the very symmetry and ceremonial ease of his syntax, he offered an analogue for the structured cosmos that was presupposed in his comic romance, and invited from his reader a rapport both with that cosmos and —in the vigor and freshness and exuberance of his prose—with its flawed and distorted and lively mirror, the human scene itself. The major thrust of romance, as of comedy, lay in the complex incongruities generated by that human creature who was at once animal and something higher. A style that would seek to be true to one dimension must present graphically and vividly the eager animal concerns, the fallibilities and contradictions, the frustrations and brief successes of the merely "actual," and, since this creature of whom we speak is a social animal, the absurdities and pleasures of local forms and manners. A style that would be true to the other dimension must present in all its promise a world of light—certain, ordered, permanent, "real." A style that can be true to *both* dimensions, however, is of the highest rarity: it must somehow at once convey all the disorderly, incoherent, fragmented caprice and impulse that mark the foreground scene, and yet assure us of something harmonious and timeless and unequivocal behind that desperate flux. In a word, it must in its very rhythms mirror the painful, joyful anomalies of what it is to be human in a world of ultimate suprahuman meaning.

As Squire Western dogs the path of Sophia from Upton, not far from the spirit in which hunter pursues hare or fox (for previous allusions to both have provided a metaphorical context), he laments "the Loss of so fine a Morning for Hunting."

> Whether Fortune, who now and then shews some Compassion in her wantonest Tricks, might not take Pity of the Squire; and as she had determined not to let him overtake his Daughter, might not resolve to make him Amends some other Way, I will not assert; but he had hardly uttered the Words just before commemorated, and two or three Oaths at their Heels, when a Pack of Hounds began to open their melodious Throats at a small Distance from them, which the Squire's Horse and his Rider both perceiving, both immediately pricked up their Ears, and the Squire crying, "She's gone, she's gone! Damn me if she is not gone!" instantly clapped Spurs to the Beast, who little needed it, having indeed the same Inclination with his Master; and now the whole Company crossing into a Corn-field, rode directly towards the Hounds, with much Hallowing and Hooping, while the poor Parson, blessing himself, brought up the Rear. (12.2)[14]

Not to analyze this period at length, although it is typical enough, the easy and elegant dignity ("commemorated" and "melodious Throats" are not entirely mock), the balanced and formal syntax, and the sure control, despite a tentativeness on the semantic level, reflect a cosmos of certainty and order that remains serene whatever the furor and mutations under its eye. The style itself, more than the casual but significant allusion to daimonic forces (of "Fortune") beyond human control or total comprehension, creates this higher dimension of Fielding's multi-leveled universe. To the other dimension he is equally faithful, however, for the contingent phrasing ("Whether ...") and the semantic tentativeness ("I will not assert") reflect a world less certain in its operations, as the shift to participial modifier ("now ... crossing") and the rapid alternation of levels of stylistic suggestiveness ("commemorated" followed by "Oaths" followed by "melodious Throats" followed by the comical equation of beast and rider) mirror the erratic and stumbling randomness of its activities. The narrative exuberance and animation are precisely balanced by the cool, benevolent detachment, and yet both are of a piece, quite indivisible, intimately linked, in every detail a stylistic emblem of the larger structure both of Fielding's comic romance and of the full cosmos it presupposed.

So, too, Fielding's settings are presented in language that, as I have suggested in my comment on Paradise Hall and elsewhere, is invested with symbolic or moral force. But setting is of less interest to him than character and it is to the role that an artful language plays in romance characterization that I should prefer to turn. A subtle analyst of style in the novel has reminded us that "Confusion about the novelist's art is likely to persist as long as we think of his use of language (or 'style') as a skill that can be distinguished from, and on occasion weighed against, his ability to create characters and actions."[15] The argument is surely sound, and clearly applies to the creation of character in romance as well. Language throughout *Tom Jones* provides a control that shapes our response to character and action, deepens and subtilizes it. When we are introduced to the heroine, for example, she is presented to us first through the beguiling haze of the pastoral sublime and only then brought down to earth; for *of course* this is precisely the aura that surrounds the loved object for the young lover, and we are invited to share that dazed adoration before we see that its object (as in all, or surely most such cases) is, after all, merely a human being not a goddess.

The creative use of language to surround characters with an aura of implicit "meaning" occurs at a great variety of levels: in the diction of the persons themselves, for instance, whether it be the elevated and somewhat stilted poesy that properly appertains to a world of young love, or the arrogance (and servility) of office that appears in Mrs. Deborah Wilkins, or the ignorant and vital localism of Western, or the sophisticated ignorance of his urban sister—all are given a characteristic language and intonation. Or minor characters may appear with a jargon of office—medicine, law, soldiering—that marks the human being displaced by function in his official capacity. The narrator himself sometimes echoes such a jargon for ironic effect, as in the discrepancy that is felt between the minor poaching of Black George and the stately, undiscriminating legal voice that condemns it: "This Hare he had basely and barbarously knocked on the Head, against the Laws of the Land..." (3.10).

The shifting perspectives signaled by the mimetic "voices" of the Narrator I have treated elsewhere;[16] but it may be added that Fielding himself called attention, in the prefatory chapter of his last book to this "personation" of different characters—meaning, I think, not the characters of his romance, but the "voices" employed in narration—such as, for instance, the voice of the Contemplative Man (see above, Chapter 3, on Allworthy's meditative diction), of the Institutional Moralist, of the Fair Reader or the Town-Lady or the Prude, of the Skeptic and (rarely) of the Sentimentalist. The point-of-view remains firmly that of the narrator, but by rendering a given passage in the "voice" of the type-figure who lies behind a traditional attitude or posture he achieves a most subtle variation upon straight narrative, a variation that once again conveys implicit "meaning." Just one example, the mimetic "voice" of a young girl in love, "personated" in the course of the narration itself:

> Thus his Backwardness, his Shunning her, his Coldness and his Silence, were the forwardest, the most diligent, the warmest, and most eloquent Advocates; and wrought so violently on her sensible and tender Heart, that she soon felt for him all those gentle Sensations which are consistent with a virtuous and elevated female Mind—In short, all which Esteem, Gratitude, and Pity, can inspire in such, towards an agreeable Man—Indeed, all which the nicest Delicacy can allow—In a Word,—she was in Love with him to Distraction. (5.6)

Fielding slips easily into these "personations," and one may not even consciously notice them—indeed, I cannot find that anyone *has* previously noticed them—but they function most effectively to join the precisely appropriate feeling-tone to the situation that the Narrator is describing. This happy device is known to rhetoric as the figure of *prosopopoeia*, the "counterfeiting" of universal character-types and their modes of speech, and it is a versatile tool in the hands of a Narrator who is not a *persona* (in the modern sense) but a Narrator, because he can drop the mask as quickly as he has lifted it.

If Fielding followed the rhetorical and the romance mode in the creation of typological characters, he also found the individual in the type—the distinctive and idiosyncratic features that gave a personal stamp to his representative personages. Indeed, he rather prided himself—and with reason—upon this traditional Renaissance skill, and lest the careless critic overlook it buttonholed him ("my good Reptile") in the prefatory chapter to the tenth book, to explain what he was doing. Squire Western is perhaps his finest achievement in this distinguished art, and I may conclude my remarks upon the interrelationship of style and character with one note on this *senex iratus*. Fielding's additive style, with its numerous qualifying subordinate phrases and clauses, its habit of *correctio* and parenthesis, could precisely emblematize the judicious and balanced mind of the Narrator; but, with a slight distortion it could also create a startlingly different effect, the sense of a confused and disorderly mind in such as Squire Western. Consider this narrative account of Western, when Sophia has asked to be excused from supper (italics mine):

> To this Request likewise the Squire agreed, *though* not without some Reluctance; *for* he scarce ever permitted her to be out of his Sight, *unless* when he was engaged with his Horses, Dogs, or Bottle. *Nevertheless* he yielded to the Desire of his Daughter, *though* the poor Man was, at the same Time, obliged to avoid his own Company, (*if* I may so express myself) *by* sending for a neighbouring Farmer to sit with him. (4.10)

There we have in little a perfectly achieved syntactical emblem of Squire Western's mind, bouncing from alternative to alternative, as whim and wish and impulse direct.

To turn to the question of theme: rhetoric and the arts of style were, of course, central to the embodiment and articulation of moral values in narrative, whether the artist's desire was to enunciate themes directly or to mask them skillfully behind an apparently value-free surface or to link them with a particular feeling-tone or to complicate them with all the ambiguities and ambivalencies that have forever attended human moral conduct and human moral judgment. This by no means exhausts the range of possibilities: it merely suggests some of the ways in which style is important to theme.

I have said that both comedy and romance required that the adequate reader or auditor should have in advance some comprehension of the truths that the work of art was concerned to express. Since both depended upon a double realm of value—the world of flux with its distinctively human claims and the world of order which could alone bestow significance upon those claims—the possibilities for confusion or ambiguity were great. And the wisest authors made this itself part of their theme. The reader had to be given access to an order of judgment that placed in its proper perspective all the hilarious and painful distortions and perversions of truth in the world of the actual; but he could not be allowed to forget that it was *he* who was being described. *Tu quoque, lector!*

Fielding is not shy about direct statements; but, most often, his beguiling habit is to phrase them humorously, tentatively, or paradoxically:

> THERE are a Set or Religious, or rather Moral Writers, who teach that Virtue is the certain Road to Happiness, and Vice to Misery in this World. A very wholsome and comfortable Doctrine, and to which we have but one Objection, namely, That it is not true. (15.1)

Equally typical, however, is the masking of the Narrator's judgment behind an apparently insouciant "report" of moral obliquity, *wertfrei* and unconcerned, as in Fielding's treatment of the Molly Seagrim episode (of which I shall speak). This has confused a few modern readers accustomed to moral discourse in direct and explicit language; but, as I have perhaps sufficiently argued, Fielding's world is never value-free, and a judgment is always implicit, even when it is conveyed entirely in stylistic terms, in negative metaphors and images. (Or judgment may be structurally implied, as in the fact that the sword which Jones buys for a guinea from the sergeant, to defend his "honor," is never employed in such honorable acts as the rescue of the Old Man or of Mrs. Waters, but only in the brawl with Fitzpatrick.)

The ligature of theme and feeling-tone (to continue with the ways in which style possesses thematic significance) is, however, a more problematic matter. One could perhaps judge, in authors whose moral universe differs from our own, which values they were certain of by those that they could treat playfully or enigmatically, and which values lacked public or even private validation by those that they felt the need to treat with a rhetoric of pathos. In *Tom Jones* this rhetoric of pathos, at least in its most obvious forms, is largely confined to the speeches of the characters and seldom enters into the diction of the Narrator. But the long description by Mrs. Miller (13.8) of the "moving" scene ("I protest I was never more affected in my Life") in the little family of Anderson, Jones's amateur highwayman, is surely intended to offer reinforcement to the reader's sense that Jones has behaved properly in pardoning him. As we have seen, however, this was something of a special case and one that Fielding himself had doubts about, hence it invited a heightened "validating" appeal to sentiment, i.e., recourse to a rhetoric of pathos. Samuel Richardson, as pure bourgeois in a world (still) of aristocratic public values, exploited this pathetic diction much more needfully and obsessively, and was beyond question more skillful at it than Fielding.

Fielding's normal treatment of sentiment was that of classic comedy and the romance, sympathetic but detached: "*Sophia* then returned to her Chamber of Mourning, where she indulged herself (if the Phrase may be allowed me) in all the Luxury of tender Grief" (7.5). Yet, as with the tradition in which he wrote, he could achieve a delicate undercurrent of unstrained pathos in his comic portraits, visible for instance in the very human compound of wintry reminiscence and self-delusion that marks Mrs. Western's confidence to Sophia:

> *Sophy*, you know I love you, and can deny you nothing. You know the Easiness of my Nature; I have not always been so easy. I have been formerly thought cruel; by the Men I mean. I was called the cruel *Parthenissa*. I have broke many a Window that has had Verses to the cruel *Parthenissa* in it. *Sophy*, I was never so handsome as you, and yet I had something of you formerly. I am a little altered. Kingdoms and States, as *Tully Cicero* says in his Epistles, undergo Alterations, and so must the human Form. (17.4)

"I am a little altered"! In such a phrase Fielding could achieve a Shakespearian pathos that the Richardsonians would never know. It was, however, in the condemnation of such unsocial and "inhuman" vices as malice and hypocrisy that Fielding most typically invested theme with a high level of feeling, not the less potent for assuming the steady march of the classical moralist:

> Vice hath not, I believe, a more abject Slave; Society produces not a more odious Vermin; nor can the Devil receive a Guest more worthy of him, nor possibly more welcome to him, than a Slanderer. The World, I am afraid, regards not this Monster with half the Abhorrence which he deserves, and I am more afraid to assign the Reason of this criminal Lenity shewn towards him; yet it is certain that the Thief looks innocent in the Comparison; nay, the Murderer himself can seldom stand in Competition with his Guilt.... (11.1)

And finally, on the question of articulating theme in narrative, we have the exploitation of literary conventions and literary language to complicate a theme with all the difficult ambiguities that attend moral judgment upon human actions. Tom's famous (or infamous) retirement into the bushes with Molly Seagrim on the heels of his avowal of eternal loyalty to Sophia, is presented in linguistic terms as a collision of the elevated pastoral style (reminiscent of Sidney's *Arcadia*) with a controlled version of the "low" style—"for here we have no temple but the wood, no assembly but horn-beasts."[17] So Cervantes follows the pastoral elevation of Marcella's tale with the episode of Rosinante seeking to mount the Galician mares, and Shakespeare neighbors the lyric love-duet of Romeo and Juliet with the calculated bawdry of Mercutio. The world of high idealism and constancy in love is perhaps no less "actual" than the natural world of animal need— and fiction that ignores either of these poles is inadequate to our full experience of the human situation—but their immediate and jarring stylistic juxtaposition offers a pungent fictive commentary upon the eternal tension between what we are able to conceive as our "best" selves and what we perform as our "worst" selves. Tom's unfortunate choice between the two selves can swell the institutional moralist with the joy of spiritual pride; most of us may feel merely rueful; but only the reader who does not understand Fielding will take it as an endorsement by the author. The narrator calls attention to the fact that Tom was now in the power of wine as well as of youthful passion; but his long simile of rutting animals (5.11) makes its own implicit but severe stylistic judgment upon a mindless *amor ferinus*. The involutions of syntax and diction in that simile, however, strongly figure forth the profound complexities involved in offering, as I have put it, a holiday from legalism (and maintaining sympathy for a drunken and lecherous young man) while firmly asserting the ultimate rightness of the Law that condemns the action and rendering an unsentimental judgment upon the displacement of a worthy love by mere animal need. In the final analysis, this very complex achievement is an achievement of style.

And so we come to the Narrator himself. I shall not repeat an argument made elsewhere, that Fielding as narrator functions very much like a "character" in his own romance; however, it is certain that *persona*, in its modern sense, is not adequate to describe his role. He provides the wise and resonant moral center of the narrative, the "great Sensorium" in which the full range of competing moral and personal claims can be encompassed, and in which the precious balance between the formal demands of Law and the flexibility of particular applications that we call Equity can be maintained. More narrowly, his stylistic function is to establish an equable norm of easy discourse, from which any departures will signal the adequate reader that a shift in attention or "set" is required. The tradition of decorum offered him various levels of style that automatically conveyed such signals; and the great panoply of rhetorical schemes and figures could function in a like way, as Fielding's "personated" voices would also invite from the reader delicate shifts in response. The modalities of Fielding's irony have justly received attention from a number of commentators; but that notable and characteristic feature of both his fictional and nonfictional works is only one of an astonishing array of verbal controls through which he subtly worked to shape his reader's responses and attitudes. Both the "disjunctive" controls that ask the reader to stand aside and reflect, to look upon the human comedy with that impersonal detachment which alone perhaps can savor its persistent patterns, and the "conjunctive" invitations to personal involvement and an outgoing sympathy—both contribute in equal measure to the fully realized world that Fielding's language conjures up for us. And it is the ever-inventive freshness of foreground stir inextricably joined with the never-failing formal control that can be said to give us in *Tom Jones* both the sense of a faithful mimesis, as Fielding understood the term (assuredly not in the limited Auerbachian sense) and, most necessarily, the luminous apprehension as well of a higher, more uniform and constant order of truth.

Perhaps it is time, however, to descend to particular analysis; and I shall conclude this comment upon style in *Tom Jones* with a slightly more detailed examination of a single passage—chosen really for its "averageness" as an example of his narrative style, rather than for any spectacular qualities— because I wish to suggest that almost any passage taken at random from *Tom Jones* will display an equal fullness and complexity of texture. As I have observed, Fielding followed the classical decorum of the hierarchical levels of style, the Plain for simple narrative of action, the Middle for more complex narrative tasks, and the Grand (only in parody) for such epideictic celebrations as the introduction of Sophia. To this familiar triad, he (in effect) subjoined a fourth level that I have elsewhere called "the elegant Middle style," less figurative than the Grand, but more artfully schematic than the narrative Middle style. This variant is the norm of Fielding's nonfictional essays and of the introductory essays in *Tom Jones* (it is signaled, for instance, by such a word as "eleemosynary"). The ordinary narrative Middle style, however, provides the ground bass to his numerous melodic variations; and it is a passage in this vein, the narrative norm, that I have chosen to examine.

It concerns Sophia's situation, as we find her in the ninth chapter of the seventh book, preparing to escape from the home where she has been so beleaguered by her father and aunt. Squire Western has, however, just made her a present of a large bank-bill, in celebration of his sister's departure, and this unexpected tenderness gives rise to a conflict in Sophia's gentle heart (I have taken two paragraphs, but have indented each new sentence to facilitate analysis and to suggest the variation in sentence-length that is in itself so typical a feature of Fielding's style):

The latter Part of Mr. *Western's* Behaviour had so strong an Effect on the tender Heart of *Sophia*, that it suggested a Thought to her, which not all the Sophistry of her politic Aunt, nor all the Menaces of her Father had ever once brought into her Head.
She reverenced her Father so piously, and loved him so passionately, that she had scarce ever felt more pleasing Sensations, than what arose from the Share she frequently had of contributing to his Amusement; and sometimes, perhaps, to higher Gratifications; for he never could contain the Delight of hearing her commended, which he had the Satisfaction of hearing almost every Day of her Life.
The Idea, therefore, of the immense Happiness she should convey to her Father by her Consent to this Match, made a strong Impression on her Mind.
Again, the extreme Piety of such an Act of Obedience, worked very forcibly, as she had a very deep Sense of Religion.
Lastly, when she reflected how much she herself was to suffer, being indeed to become little less than a Sacrifice, or a Martyr, to filial Love and Duty, she felt an agreeable Tickling in a certain little Passion, which tho' it bears no immediate Affinity either to Religion or Virtue, is often so kind as to lend great Assistance in executing the Purposes of both.

*Sophia* was charmed with the Contemplation of so heroic an Action, and began to compliment herself with much premature Flattery, when *Cupid*, who lay hid in her Muff, suddenly crept out, and like *Punchinello* in a Puppet-shew, kicked all out before him.
In Truth (for we scorn to deceive our Reader, or to vindicate the Character of our Heroine, by ascribing her Actions to supernatural Impulse) the Thoughts of her beloved *Jones*, and some Hopes (however distant) in which he was very particularly concerned, immediately destroyed all which filial Love, Piety and Pride had, with their joint Endeavours, been labouring to bring about.

We need not pause for long over the lexical stratum: Fielding's vocabulary is characteristically uncomplicated but not undignified ("sophistry," "filial," "affinity," though not *recherché* are perhaps above the level of unbuttoned discourse). His language, like his syntax, creates in this typical instance of his Middle Style a norm of easy dignity. It will be noted that, grammatically, the proportion of intransitive to transitive verbs is greater at the beginning and ending of the passage, and the subjects of these verbs begin as abstractions ("part," "it," "sophistry," "menaces") and so conclude ("thought" and "hopes," "filial love, piety and pride"), whereas in the middle section we have "she" repeated eight times and then "Sophia" as the subject in the climactic sentence. The effect upon the reader is of movement from a "frame" of surrounding impersonal fact to a focused and particular concentration upon Sophia's personal psychomachia and then out to general fact once again. At this point we may merely observe in passing that, at the phonological level, the sonorous norm seems here to be established by a predominance of open vowels and nasal consonants: thus when the plosives of "tickling" and "kicked" appear, they forcibly command attention.

At the syntactic level, Fielding's basic structures would have been called hypotactic (or subordinating), with numerous "additive" dependent clauses; but within this norm, there are also two notable instances of coordinating elements, namely, the isocolon of "not all the Sophistry of her politic Aunt, nor all the Menaces of her Father" and of "She reverenced her Father so piously, and loved him so passionately," both occurring near the opening of the passage and, as deviations from the norm, inviting (subliminally perhaps) the reader's attention to a new proposition or "plot." As with Fielding's essayistic style, this narrative style exhibits a committed or premeditated syntax that knows where it is going, but that is "looser" than the Ciceronian, marked by linear addition (especially qualification and parenthesis) rather than by periodicity. The numerous logical connectives ("for," "therefore") and linking adverbs ("Again," "lastly"), like the initial paragraph link to the preceding events ("The latter Part of Mr. *Western's* Behaviour"), are typical, and help to account for the ease with which the reader follows Fielding's narrative despite the complexities of his hypotactic syntax and (at another level) of his overall plot. Like the sonority of his prose, the linking effect of the numerous connectives contributes to the disarming sense of easy, graceful flow.

I shall pass over the effective rhetorical schemata and tropes of this passage, having elsewhere paid my tribute to the shrines of Aristotle and Quintilian, and move directly to the semantic level. As the preceding observations have begun to suggest, these two paragraphs (as so often in *Tom Jones*) create a little "plot" of their own, with a conflict initiated, complicated and amplified, and finally resolved, ending in the defeat of the forces that would threaten the desired conclusion. We begin with the initial "suspense" of an unidentified "Thought" that is not fully explained until the third sentence, as Fielding (characteristically) holds us off by sketching in the context, in his second sentence. The sophistry of Sophia's aunt and the menace of her father have *not*, we are told, initiated the "Thought," and therefore these plot directors momentarily fade from central focus. Indeed, with the second sentence we are invited to shift our established perspective and see Squire Western now, not as tyrannical parent but as the object of reverence and love. In this context, Sophia's temptation (appealing to her fatal "flaw") is to renounce Jones and accept Blifil for the happiness it would cause her father. The idea is subjected to a *divisio*, with a gradation from this filial devotion through the supporting effect of Sophia's inherently religious nature, to the support offered by a very human (and humanizing) weakness, her pride. This weakness, which makes Sophia a creature not too good for human nature's daily food, is softened and extenuated, however, both at the lexical level ("an agreeable Tickling in a certain little Passion") and at the semantic level, where the narrator points out mildly that Pride "is often so kind" as to assist even the much weightier general purposes of religion and virtue. But as Sophia is enjoying the metaphorical anticipation of her "martyrdom," the equivalent of the romance warrior's "heroic Action," a sudden peripeteia occurs: for Eros (hidden in her muff, the surrogate metonymy of Sophia's sexuality) creeps out and, like Punch, kicks "all out before him" —the conclusion of our little struggle. (And, although treated by the narrator with benign amusement, Sophia's "struggle" is given greater local intensity by the numerous superlatives, the repetition of "very," and the emphasis of such words as "strong," "extreme," "forcibly," "deep," and so on.) Having concluded his "action," Fielding provides the generalizing comment that locates it and refers it to a more universal paradigm. But the reader observes that, despite this ordering and relating to a larger extratextual world, the ultimate resolution is by no means one of ethical simplicity: for the "enemies" to Sophia's love for Tom include a morally mixed group of "filial love, piety and pride," here personified as laboring to bring about her marriage to Blifil. Now, both filial love and deep religious feeling are unquestionably strong positives in Fielding's universe of discourse; and the "conclusion," therefore, is somewhat askew, ambiguous and equivocal.

In this, however, our tiny drama actually joins with the semantic tenor of *Tom Jones* as a whole, despite the latter's formally satisfying conclusion. For the troubling conflict between the forces of (even benign) Law, with its coercive religious and familial bonds of love, and the equally potent youthful need for self-realization and self-definition *is* Fielding's story. Moreover, as he sees that Pride is opposed to Grace (although it may serve the latter), so too does he see that Grace must always confront a vital, recalcitrant, imperfect (but not, in Fielding, fatedly heinous) human Nature. The narrator tells us that he will not vindicate his heroine's character by supposing that a "supernatural Impulse" led her to resist prideful temptation. This is in tune with other determined eschewals of the romance use of the "marvelous"; but, like the little plot just rehearsed, in which the word "piety" takes on both positive and negative overtones, Fielding's phrase suggests an ambivalence toward "personal" or evangelical approaches to supernaturalism itself—an ambivalence which appears more than once within the overarching frame of his altogether sincere and heartfelt depiction of an ordered providential universe.

\* \* \*

When Alexander Pope defended that great *Urquell* of the romance tradition, the *Odyssey*, against the judgment of Longinus that, as a "comic" epic, it must belong to the decline of Homer's old age, he argued the necessity of understanding "the nature of the piece and the intent of its author"; as an epic dealing with "common life," the *Odyssey*, he said, "still remains perfect in its kind."

> From the Nature of the Poem, we shall form an Idea of the *Style*. The diction is to follow the images, and to take its colour from the complexion of the thoughts. Accordingly the Odyssey is not always cloath'd in the majesty of verse proper to Tragedy, but sometimes descends into the plainer Narrative, and sometimes even to that familiar dialogue essential to Comedy. However, where it cannot support a sublimity, it always preserves a dignity, or at least a propriety.[18]

And he added, "There is a real beauty in an easy, pure, perspicuous description even of a *low action*." Pope might almost have been sketching out a paradigm of the comic epic in prose: he called for variations in style, praised the "fable" of the *Odyssey* above that of the tragic *Iliad*, and insisted that the former was not inferior in its depiction of "manners" simply because it dealt with a man "struggling with misfortunes and on a level with the meanest of mankind." The scenes of the *Odyssey*, he declared, "are generally of the comic kind; banquets, revels, sports, loves, and the pursuit of a woman."[19]

Perhaps this conception—the Renaissance and Augustan, not the Romantic conception—of the *Odyssey* helps to illuminate Fielding's choice of an epigraph: Horace's paraphrase of the opening of Homer's "comic" epic, *Mores hominum multorum vidit*.[20] But, if he truly planned an Odyssean prose-epic, he could not have escaped the fundamental challenge that such a mighty work presented. As Pope observed: "Indeed the true reason that so few Poets have imitated *Homer* in these lower parts, has been the extreme difficulty of preserving that mixture of Ease and Dignity essential to them.... *Homer* in his lowest narrations or speeches is ever easy, flowing, copious, clear and harmonious."[21] That Fielding's genius was equal, and more than equal, to this extraordinary artistic task has been the burden of my commentary. The uniquely dignified and flowing and flexible instrument of language that he forged to meet the challenge of a comic epic in prose remains among the supreme achievements of the world's literary art. And Henry Fielding remains one of those very few masters in all of Western literature whose luck and genius could run high enough (in Yeats's phrase) to reach

> To gradual Time's last gift, a written speech
> Wrought of high laughter, loveliness and ease.

# NOTES

NOTES TO CHAPTER I

[1] As Arthur Johnston observes, even the later eighteenth-century antiquarians "wrote at times of romances as though they all conformed to one pattern" (*Enchanted Ground: The Study of Medieval Romance in the Eighteenth Century* [London, 1964], p. 11). See also the useful collection, *Novel and Romance 1700-1800: A Documentary Record*, ed. Ioan Williams (London, 1970).

[2] Ben Edwin Perry, *The Ancient Romances: A Literary-Historical Account of Their Origins* (Berkeley and Los Angeles, 1967), p. 45. One might add that, as there are splendid and poor romances, so are there spendid and poor epics. The *word* "epic" does not automatically bestow literary quality surpassing that of romance—Blackmore's *King Arthur* and Bailey's *Festus* have been called "epics."

[3] *Don Quixote*, 1.4.20 (1.47); and see E. C. Riley, *Cervantes's Theory of the Novel* (Oxford, 1962), pp. 49 ff. This was a commonplace of continental criticism from at least the time of the great sixteenth-century Italian critics, Giangiorgio Trissino and Giraldi Cinthio, seconded by Torquato Tasso (J. C. Scaliger, who disagreed, did at least anticipate Sir Philip Sidney in seeing the *Aethiopica* of Heliodorus as an epic model). These critics were followed by López Pinciano in Spain and by many others, on through the influential *Traité du poème épique* (Paris, 1675) of René Le Bossu. There were counter-arguments, of course (see H. T. Swedenberg, Jr., *The Theory of the Epic in England, 1650-1800* [Berkeley and Los Angeles, 1944], pp. 155 ff., *et passim*); but clearly Fielding was not at all singular or devious in his argument.

[4] I follow the sound presentation of Homer Goldberg. "Comic Prose Epic or Comic Romance: The Argument of the Preface to *Joseph Andrews*," *PQ*, 43 (1964), 193-215.

[5] Walter R. Davis, *Idea and Act in Elizabethan Fiction* (Princeton, 1969), p. 44. See also the very interesting work by Diana Spearman, *The Novel and Society* (London, 1966).

[6] Robert Scholes and Robert Kellogg, *The Nature of Narrative* (New York, 1966), a landmark study that most ably postulates, if it does not altogether maintain, a "Copernican" view of the history of fiction. See also, of course, Northrop Frye, *Anatomy of Criticism* (Princeton, 1957), pp. 303-4, *et passim*. And if one can penetrate its horrid Romantic Hegelianism, Georg Lukács' early work, *Die Theorie des Romans* (trans. Anne Bostock, as *The Theory of the Novel*, Cambridge, Mass., 1971), is endlessly suggestive, as well as endlessly wrong.

[7] *A Preface to Paradise Lost* (London, 1942), p. 1.

[8] *Joseph Andrews*, Preface; ed. Martin C. Battestin (Oxford, 1967), p. 4. *Clélie* and *Artamène, ou le Grand Cyrus* by Madeleine de Scudéry; *Cléopâtre* and *Cassandre* by Gauthier de Costes de la Calprenède; *Astrée* by Honoré d'Urfé.

[9] *The History of Romances* (Paris, 1670; trans. Stephen Lewis, London, 1715), in Ioan Williams, p. 53.

[10] See John J. Richetti, *Popular Fiction before Richardson: Narrative Patterns 1700-1739* (Oxford, 1969), for a responsible study of the sociological implications of this subliterary genre.

[11] John J. O'Connor, *Amadis de Gaule and Its Influence on Elizabethan Literature* (New Brunswick, 1970), p. 58.

[12] Fielding's relationship to such earlier comic romances, and thereby implicitly to a larger tradition, has been well argued by Sheridan Baker, in "Henry Fielding's Comic Romances," *Papers of the Michigan Academy of Science, Arts, and Letters*, 45 (1960), 411-19, and in other essays; and Homer Goldberg has, in *The Art of Joseph Andrews* (Chicago, 1969), studied the influence upon that work of Cervantes, Lesage, Scarron, and Marivaux.

[13] *Rambler* 4 (31 March 1750); *Yale Edition of the Works of Samuel Johnson*, 3.19; my italics.

[14] Ian Watt, *The Rise of the Novel* (London, 1957), p. 205: "Emma Bovary pays involuntary tribute to the way in which the novel's access to the inner life gives it a more pervasive and enduring sway than the romance, and one which is much more difficult either to escape or to assess. As far as this sway in concerned, indeed, the question of literary quality is not of first importance." Since the sway of the romance endured for almost two millennia, it does seem a trifle early to speak of the "more enduring" sway of bourgeois realism: but that it has been more "pervasive" is unquestionable.

[15] Some preliminary observations are offered in "Augustan Prose Fiction and the Romance Tradition," to appear in the *Papers* of the Third David Nichol Smith Memorial Seminar, held at Canberra in 1973.

[16] In Ioan Williams, p. 47.

[17] Gertrude R. Levy, *The Sword from the Rock: An Investigation into the Origins of Epic Literature and the Development of the Hero* (London, 1953).

[18] See Perry, *The Ancient Romances*, Chapters 1-4.

[19] How lamely is made clear in Dieter Mehl's vigorous reassessment of familiar classifications, in *The Middle English Romances of the Thirteenth and Fourteenth Centuries* (London, 1969), pp. 30 ff.

[20] See R. S. Crane, "The Vogue of *Guy of Warwick* from the Close of the Middle Ages to the Romantic Revival," *PMLA*, 30 (1915), 125-94.

[21] *Don Quixote*, 1.6; trans. Motteux-Ozell, 5th edn., 1.43.

[22] Walter R. Davis, in the composite volume containing a valuable contribution by Richard A. Lanham, *Sidney's Arcadia* (New Haven, 1965), p. 168.

[23] Davis, p. 174. On the "genre" of the *Arcadia*, there is an intelligent commentary by Alan D. Isler, "Heroic Poetry and Sidney's Two *Arcadias*," *PMLA*, 83 (1968), 368-79.

[24] "Avis au lecteur," prefatory to *Faramond* (Paris, 1661-70), cited in Vivienne Mylne, *The Eighteenth-Century French Novel* (Manchester, 1965), p. 22.

[25] "To the Reader," *Cassandra*, trans. Sir Charles Cotterell (London, 1664), sig. A4v; italics reversed.

[26] See Arthur L. Cooke, "Henry Fielding and the Writers of Heroic Romance," *PMLA*, 62 (1947), 984-94.

[27] As emblematic of this historical reassessment (and as a personal act of *pietas*), I may cite two representative works of profound scholarship, D. W. Robertson, Jr., *A Preface to Chaucer: Studies in Medieval Perspectives* (Princeton, 1962), and Jean H. Hagstrum, *The Sister Arts: The Tradition of Literary Pictorialism and English Poetry from Dryden to Gray* (Chicago, 1958).

NOTES TO CHAPTER 2

[1] *The Hero with a Thousand Faces* (2nd edn., Princeton, Bollingen Series 17, 1968). Campbell's triad is more compendious and more universally recognizable in Western narrative than the somewhat elaborate schemata of motifs set forth by Lord Raglan in his study of the Hero and by Vladimir Propp in his morphology of the folktale.

[2] See Martin C. Battestin, "Fielding: The Argument of Design," in *The Providence of Wit* (Oxford, 1974), pp. 141-63; and Aubrey Williams, "Interpositions of Providence and the Design of Fielding's Novels," *South Atlantic Quarterly*, 70 (1971), 265-86. William W. Combs offers a useful concise comment upon the tradition of *fortuna* in "The Return to Paradise Hall: An Essay on Tom Jones," *South Atlantic Quarterly*, 67 (1968), 419-36.

[3] Lodge, *Complete Works* (Glasgow, 1883), 1.9. For the topos of Nature and Fortune, see also the opening of Lyly's *Euphues* or, for that matter, the dedication of Bacon's *Advancement of Learning* to King James.

[4] Or as J. H. Van den Berg puts it: "if adulthood is invisible, youth lives in a fog" (*The Changing Nature of Man* [New York, 1961], p. 48).

[5] S. L. Goldberg, *The Classical Temper: A Study of James Joyce's Ulysses* (London, 1961), p. 264, speaking of Joyce's relationship to his characters.

[6] Eric Rothstein, *Restoration Tragedy: Form and the Process of Change* (Madison, Wisc., 1967), p. 8.

[7] *A Natural Perspective: The Development of Shakespearean Comedy and Romance* (New York, 1965), p. 27.

[8] Cf. my essay on "The 'Digressive' Tales in Fielding's *Tom Jones* and the Perspective of Romance," in the Festschrift for Curt Zimansky, *Philological Quarterly*, 1975; and see also, on "the enclosed self," Morris Golden, *Fielding's Moral Psychology* (Amherst, Mass., 1966).

[9] Which Fielding may suggest in his description of the licentious troop of soldiers that Tom joins: "This brought to our Heroe's Mind the Custom which he had read of among the *Greeks* and *Romans*, of indulging, on certain Festivals and solemn Occasions, the Liberty to Slaves, of using an uncontrouled Freedom of Speech towards their Masters" (7.11).

[10] Frye, *A Natural Perspective*, p. 115.

[11] *The English Novel: Form and Function* (New York, 1953), p. 80; an insight finely elaborated by Frederick W. Hilles, "Art and Artifice in *Tom Jones*," in the John Butt Festschrift, *Imagined Worlds*, ed. Maynard Mack and Ian Gregor (London, 1968), pp. 91-110.

[12] "The Composition of 'Don Quixote,'" in *Cervantes across the Centuries*, ed. Angel Flores and M. J. Bernadete (New York, 1947), pp. 56-93; p. 57. This valuable essay also comments upon the *orden desordenada* of Baroque art, which "hides its strict order in a disorder that imitates nature ..." (p. 56).

[13] See Robert M. Durling, *The Figure of the Poet in Renaissance Epic* (Cambridge, Mass., 1965), pp. 126-29, *et passim*, for the relevant historical context of Fielding's image of the *deus artifex*.

[14] *Orlando Furioso*, 13.19, of Bradamante and her guide (trans. Sir John Harington [London, 1591], 23.11):
> A wandring pesaunt twas her hap to finde,
> To him she doth betake the horses spare,
> Though of the wayes they both vnskilfull are.

[15] *Aspects of the Novel* (London, 1927), p. 132.

[16] Shakespeare's *Pericles*, 5.3.90.

[17] "The Concept of Plot and the Plot of *Tom Jones*," in *Critics and Criticism*, ed. R. S. Crane (Chicago, 1952), pp. 616-47; p. 637.

[18] Walter R. Davis, *Sidney's Arcadia*, p. 163. The most influential source for this examination of the soul in prison would be, of course, Boethius.

[19] Lodge, *Complete Works*, 1.59, 90.

[20] *The Comedy of Dante Alighieri: Cantica II: Purgatory*, 30.136-38; trans. Dorothy L. Sayers (Harmondsworth, 1955), p. 311.

[21] *Shakespeare's Festive Comedy* (Princeton, 1959), pp. 125-26.

[22] *Anatomy of Criticism*, p. 181.

[23] See, for instance, Peter L. Thorslev, Jr., "Incest as Romantic Symbol," *Comparative Literature Studies*, 2 (1965), 41-58. Barry D. Bort's "Incest Theme in Tom Jones," *American N & Q*, 3 (1965), 83-84, treats the topic in terms of an antiheroic parody of classical motifs, which is mistaken, but is at least nearer the mark than the Edwardian moral huffings of Frank Kermode on the subject, in "Richardson and Fielding," *Cambridge Journal*, 4 (1950), 106-14.

[24] *Shakespeare's Festive Comedy*, p. 245.

[25] See John J. O'Connor, *Amadis de Gaule*, pp. 54 and 122.

[26] Heliodorus, *Aethiopica*, 7.8; trans. Thomas Underdowne, ed. Charles Whibley (London, 1895), p. 182.

[27] Samuel Lee Wolff, *The Greek Romances in Elizabethan Prose Fiction* (New York, 1912), p. 188. Although stuffed with bourgeois "moral" judgments intolerable to the world of romance, Wolff's study is nevertheless scholarly and useful.

[28] Luigi Pulci, *Il Morgante Maggiore*, stanza 49; translated somewhat lamely by Lord Byron: "Good is rewarded, and chastised the ill, / Which the Lord never faileth to fulfil" (*Works of Byron* [London, 1832], 11.233).

[29] Respectively, Chrétien de Troyes, *Yvain* (trans. W. W. Comfort, p. 238); *Amadis de Gaule*, 2.21 (trans. Anthony Munday, 2.166); Ariosto, *Orlando Furioso*, 18.77 (trans. Harington, 18.31, p. 139); and Thomas Lodge, *Rosalynde* (in *Complete Works*, 1.59).

[30] Letter of G. T. to H. W., prefatory to *The Adventures of Master F.J.*, ed. C. T. Prouty, in Gascoigne's *A Hundreth Sundrie Flowers* (Columbia, Missouri, 1942), p. 50.

[31] *The Hero with a Thousand Faces*, p. 28.

[32] Dorothy L. Sayers, trans. *The Comedy of Dante Alighieri: Cantica II: Purgatory*, p. 293.

[33] *Amadis de Gaule*, 4.26; trans. Anthony Munday (final version, 1619), 4.119.

NOTES TO CHAPTER 3

[1] *Complete Works of John Lyly*, ed. R. W. Bond (Oxford, 1902), 2.13.

[2] The time-scheme, originally worked out by Frederick S. Dickson, can be found in Wilbur L. Cross, *The History of Henry Fielding* (New Haven, 1918), 2.189 ff. Although the best authority on this matter, Martin C. Battestin, in his Wesleyan edition of *Tom Jones*, is skeptical of any close attention to almanacs on Fielding's part, it is pleasant enough to visualize Fielding calling out with Bottom, "A calendar, a calendar! Look in the almanac! Find out moonshine, find out moonshine"; and, since the calendar ends with the departure of the lovers for Somerset on 31 December, we are permitted to say that they mark the onset of a new year with the beginning of their new life. Manuel Schonhorn has some provocative remarks upon the time-scheme and its significance, in "Heroic Allusion in *Tom Jones*: Hamlet and the Temptations of Jesus," *Studies in the Novel*, 6 (1974), 218-27.

[3] See Mircea Eliade, *The Myth of the Eternal Return* (trans. New York, 1954).

[4] *Henry V*, prologue; cf. also "Time" as Chorus before the fifth act of *The Winter's Tale*.

[5] "Structural Techniques in Tom Jones," *Zeitschrift für Anglistik und Amerikanistik*, 7 (1959), 5-16; p. 7.

[6] *Fielding: Tom Jones* (London, 1964), p. 31.

[7] *Arcadia*, 1.2; *Complete Works*, ed. Albert Feuillerat (Cambridge, 1912-26), 1.15. On the *paradeisos*, see A. Bartlett Giamatti, *The Earthly Paradise and the Renaissance Epic* (Princeton, 1966), and Ernst Curtius, *European Literature and the Latin Middle Ages*, trans. W. R. Trask (New York, Bollingen Series 36, 1953), Chapter 10.

[8] *Paradise Lost*, 4.144-45, 223 ff., *et passim*.

[9] See Walter Davis, *Sidney's Arcadia*, pp. 61-63.

[10] *Enquiry after Happiness* (London, 1685), cited in Maren-Sofie Røstvig, *The Happy Man* (Oslo, 1954-58), 2.23.

[11] *Essays*, ed. W. P. Ker, 1.55. Cf. Butler, *Hudibras*, 1.1.325 ff., and, on the peninsular romances, *Don Quixote*, 1.2.2 (1.10).

[12] *Clitophon and Leucippe*, 1.5.

[13] *Jerusalem Delivered*, 5.63, 64; trans. Edward Fairfax ("Fourth Edition," London, 1749), pp. 109-10.

[14] Armida, in *Jerusalem Delivered*, 4.94; trans. Fairfax, p. 92.

[15] On the theme of the "quinque linea," variously glossed, but almost always beginning with sight and ending in coitus, see E. R. Curtius, *European Literature and the Latin Middle Ages*, trans. Trask, pp. 512-14; Curtius says, "From Latin poetry the theme makes its way into the vernacular poetry of the romances" (p. 513).

[16] J. F. Kermode, "The Banquet of Sense," *Bulletin of the John Rylands Library*, 44 (1961), 68-99; p. 83. See also Donald K. Anderson, Jr., "The Banquet of Love in English Drama (1595-1642)," *JEGP*, 63 (1964), 422-32, who cites, for instance, Ben Jonson's *New Inn* (3.2), in which Achilles Tatius and Heliodorus are invoked, and recalls the banquet given Clitophon by Melitte in the fifth book of *Clitophon and Leucippe*.

[17] *Venus and Adonis*, 423-26.

[18] Cf. Xenophon, *Memorabilia*, 2.1.21-33.

[19] *Jerusalem Delivered*, 17.61; trans. Fairfax, p. 386.

[20] Ruggiero, under Alcina's spell, in *Orlando Furioso*, 7.18, trans. Harington 7.17, p. 50, Bradamante, like Sophia, is searching for her lover while he is thus engaged.

[21] Mrs. Waters' "two lovely blue Eyes, whose bright Orbs flashed Lightning at their Discharge" are in the mode of Tasso's Armida: "Her humid Eyes a fiery Smile forth shot, / That like Sun-beams in silver Fountains shin'd" (*Jerusalem Delivered*, 16.18; trans. Fairfax, p. 356).

[22] *Orlando Furioso*, 7.70; trans. Harington, 7.59, p. 53.

[23] *Aeneid*, 1.748-49.

[24] Cited in John J. Richetti, *Popular Fiction before Richardson*, p. 194.

[25] Maurice Johnson has a perceptive comment (among many) upon the relevance of Southerne's play to Sophia's situation, in *Fielding's Art of Fiction* (Philadelphia, 1961), pp. 107-14.

[26] *Fielding: Tom Jones*, p. 41.

[27] Ben Jonson, *Epigrammes*, 128, "To William Roe," 6-8, 12-14; ed. Herford-Simpson, 8.81.

NOTES TO CHAPTER 4

[1] Martin Battestin, commenting upon Fielding's prefatory chapter to Book 7, cites the *locus classicus* in Epictetus: "For consider, that the playing of the Part assigned you commendably, depends upon your self. This is your Business; but the giving out of the Parts, and choosing the Actors, is not yours, but another Person's" (ed. *Tom Jones*, 1.323).

[2] Chrétien, *Arthurian Romances*, trans. W. W. Comfort, p. 279.

[3] "The Composition of 'Don Quixote,' " p. 87.

[4] Sheridan Baker, "Bridget Allworthy: The Creative Pressures of Fielding's Plot," *Papers of the Michigan Academy*, 52 (1967), 345-56; p. 356.

[5] "Preface to Shakespeare" (1765), ed. Arthur Sherbo, in the *Yale Edition of the Works*, 7.62.

[6] Lady Luxborough's letter of 1749 is cited in Frederic T. Blanchard, *Fielding the Novelist* (New Haven, 1925), p. 70; my italics. Richardson's letter of 22 February 1752, to Mrs. Donellan, is in the *Correspondence of Samuel Ricardson*, ed. Mrs. A. L. Barbauld (London, 1804), 4.60-61.

[7] Clara Reeve, in 1785, seems to have initiated the phrase that would become standard in genteel female circles, that Fielding "certainly painted human nature as *it is*, rather than as *it ought to be*" (*The Progress of Romance*, repr. Facsimile Text Society, p. 141). Regrettably, she had authority for this posture in Samuel Johnson.

[8] *The English Novel: Form and Function*, p. 67.

[9] Dr. Bruno Bettelheim, trained originally in the Freudian theory of a slow "evolutionary" development of personality, tells us that the incredibly rapid and radical character changes "both for better and worse" that he witnessed in Dachau and Buchenwald awakened him to the inadequacy of the theory in crisis-situations (*The Informed Heart: Autonomy in a Mass Age* [Glencoe, Ill., 1960], p. 14, *et passim*). The late Victorian and Edwardian notion of literary "character" clearly depended upon the conception of a crisis-free, feminine "domestic" world, in which character could "develop" smoothly and gradually, free of unseemly leaps. This was not the kind of world the romance knew.

[10] For the steps leading to the apocalyptic moment of conversion in the Puritan tradition, see George A. Starr, *Defoe and Spiritual Autobiography* (Princeton, 1965).

[11] *Henry V*, 1.1.28-29.

[12] *1 Henry IV*, 5.2.62-65; my italics. Achilles Tatius (8.17) cites the case of Themistocles as historical warrant for the "sudden transformation" in his fictive Callisthenes.

[13] "An Essay on the Knowledge of the Characters of Men," in the *Miscellanies*, ed. H. K. Miller (Oxford, 1972), 1.160.

[14] On the conception of role-playing in the Renaissance, see Walter R. Davis, *Idea and Act in Elizabethan Fiction*, pp. 45 ff.

[15] Thus, in Ariosto, when Ruggiero is converted to Christianity, he puts off his baptism and insists upon continuing to serve his "paynim" king, in order "that foolish people might not make a iest / to his reproch" and call him turncoat (*Orlando Furioso*, 25.90; trans. Harington, 25.74, p. 203). The point is several times repeated.

[16] On the latter, see G. A. Starr, *Defoe and Casuistry* (Princeton, 1971).

[17] Cf., however, Fielding's "judicial" position on this question in the *Enquiry into the Causes of the Late Increase of Robbers*, sect. 2.

[18] *Fielding and the Nature of the Novel* (Cambridge, Mass., 1968), p. 67.

[19] Ovid, *Heroides*, 7.17.

[20] See Chapter 2, note 8.

[21] *Complete Works*, 1.94.

[22] *Orlando Furioso*, Canto 10; it will be remembered that, while Ruggiero is pantingly trying to disencumber himself of his armor—at which point Ariosto ended the Tenth Canto, fearing lest his readers might be wearied! —Angelica uses her magic ring to escape in invisibility.

[23] Chrétien, *Arthurian Romances*, trans. W. W. Comfort, p. 207.

[24] Book 4; ed. Feuillerat, 2.83.

[25] Act 4, scene 1; 3rd edn., 1691, p. 37.

NOTES TO CHAPTER 5

[1] Sheldon Sacks offers a subtle analysis of the modes by which "aesthetic signals" are translated into "ethical statements" in *Fiction and the Shape of Belief* (Berkeley and Los Angeles, 1964).

[2] S. N. Eisenstadt, "Archetypal Patterns of Youth," in *The Challenge of Youth*, ed. Erik H. Erikson (New York: Anchor Books, 1965), pp. 29, 31.

[3] See Peter B. Murray, "Summer, Winter, Spring, and Autumn in *Tom Jones*," *MLN*, 76 (1961), 324-26.

[4] Peter L. Berger, *Invitation to Sociology: A Humanistic Perspective* (New York: Anchor Books, 1963), p. 145.

[5] *Shakespeare's Festive Comedy*, p. 13.

[6] On this, see Glenn W. Hatfield, *Henry Fielding and the Language of Irony* (Chicago, 1968).

[7] *Allegory: The Theory of a Symbolic Mode* (Ithaca, N.Y., 1964), pp. 224-25. Fletcher's work, some Romantic lapses apart (for allegory is also a non-Romantic mode), serves admirably as a general comment upon the "antimimetic" element in romance, and I have drawn upon it for more than one insight.

[8] For Cervantes, too, *discreción* was a major focus of moral concern: see Margaret Bates, *"Discreción" in the Works of Cervantes* (Washington, 1945). As Addison says, "Discretion does not only shew it self in Words, but in all the Circumstances of Action, and is like an Under-Agent of Providence to guide and direct us in the ordinary Concerns of Life" (*Spectator* 225; ed. Donald F. Bond, 2.375).

[9] *Richard II*, 2.1.2.

[10] *Euphues*, in *Complete Works of John Lyly*, ed. R. W. Bond, 1.187, 191.

[11] Ibid., p. 185.

[12] Sidney, *Arcadia*, 1.18; ed. Feuillerat, 1.117.

[13] *The Tempest*, 1.2.450-52.

[14] *Amadis de Gaule*, 1.26; trans. Munday, 1.167.

[15] *Orlando Furioso*, 25.31; trans. Harington, 25.25.

[16] *The Comedy: Cantica II: Purgatory*, 30.118-20, 130-32; trans. Dorothy L. Sayers, p. 310.

[17] Throughout *Tom Jones*, Fielding offers a variety of "allegories" about Love—as mere appetite, as the effect of gratitude and esteem, as a disease, a military operation, a contest with the Reason, a pursuit or hunt, and so on—that makes it quite impossible to rest easily with a single "romantic" dimension; and thus a complex metaphorical underlayer is created for the surface action.

[18] *Amadis de Gaule*, 2.15; trans. Munday, 2.100.

[19] E. H. Gombrich, *Meditations on a Hobby Horse and Other Essays on the Theory of Art* (Greenwich, Conn., 1963), p. 29.

[20] *Much Ado about Nothing*, 5.4.129-31.

[21] Escalus, in *Measure for Measure*, 2.1.298-99.

[22] *Orlando Furioso*, 30.15; trans. Harington, 30.13. Ariosto says only, "La Fortuna, che dei pazzi ha cura"; but in any case it is proverbial.

[23] Book 5; ed. Feuillerat, 2.206.

[24] See Aubrey Williams, "Congreve's *Incognita* and the Contrivances of Providence," in *Imagined Worlds*, ed. Maynard Mack and Ian Gregor (London, 1968), pp. 3-18; also his "Poetical Justice, the Contrivances of Providence, and the Works of William Congreve," *ELH*, 35 (1968), 540-65.

NOTES TO CHAPTER 6

[1] Fielding's own "short Hint of what we can do in the Sublime" (*Tom

*Jones*, 4.2) refers to the older tradition of the *rhetorical* sublime, whose concern was significant language, not vague uplift.

[2] *Complete Works*, 1.110.

[3] *Orlando Furioso*, 18.1; Harington translates (inadequately): "Although my words and verse inferiour are . . ." (p. 137).

[4] C. L. Barber, *Shakespeare's Festive Comedy*, p. 141.

[5] "Strange Relations: The Author and His Audience," in his *Facets of the Enlightenment* (Berkeley and Los Angeles, 1968), p. 298. See also, of course, Wayne C. Booth, *The Rhetoric of Fiction* (Chicago, 1961).

[6] Perry, *The Ancient Romances*, p. 184. See also Scholes and Kellogg, *The Nature of Narrative*, pp. 240 ff.

[7] *Don Quixote*, 2.61; trans. Motteux-Ozell, 4.256.

[8] As an accepted principle, "decorum" could also be treated playfully: Rosalind, disguised as the page Ganymede, in Lodge's *Rosalynde*, says, after passing some satirical comments upon women: "I keepe decorum, I speake now as I am ALIENAS page, not as I am GERISMONDS daughter" (*Complete Works*, 1.37). Or Dorastus, dressed as a shepherd to woo Fawnia, in Greene's *Pandosto*, reproves himself: "thou keepest a right *decorum*, base desires and homely attires" (*Life and Complete Works*, ed. Grosart, 4.287).

[9] *The Rhetoric of Fiction*, p. 112. On "the Implied Reader" see also the survey by Arthur Sherbo, *Studies in the Eighteenth Century Novel* (East Lansing, Mich., 1969), pp. 35-57.

[10] *Conversations with William Drummond of Hawthornden*, ed. R. F. Patterson (London, 1923), p. 2. However, as Jonas Barish points out, Jonson overlooked the language of the clownish figures, Miso and Mopsa (*Ben Jonson and the Language of Prose Comedy* [Cambridge, Mass., 1960], pp. 20 and 305n.).

[11] *Ars poetica*, 93: "yet sometimes even comedy elevates her voice." On the expansion of this hint by Donatus and later commentators, see Marvin T. Herrick, *Comic Theory in the Sixteenth Century* (Urbana, Ill., 1950), p. 216. It is an early form of the argument that levels of diction in themselves may carry meaning.

[12] See my *Essays on Fielding's Miscellanies* (Princeton, 1961), pp. 150 ff. On the "informal" elements in Fielding's style, see William B. Coley, "The Background of Fielding's Laughter," *ELH*, 26 (1959), 229-52, and William J. Farrell, "Fielding's Familiar Style," *ELH*, 34 (1967), 65-77. Among other critical studies, besides that by Robert Alter, previously mentioned, which are warmly alive to Fielding's stylistic mastery, may be mentioned Andrew Wright, *Henry Fielding: Mask and Feast* (Berkeley and Los Angeles, 1965), and C. J. Rawson, *Henry Fielding and the Augustan Ideal under Stress* (London, 1972).

[13] "Some Functions of Rhetoric in *Tom Jones*," *PQ*, 45 (1966), 209-35; pp. 215-16.

[14] Fielding may have remembered Addison's *Freeholder* 3, which, in mocking the Jacobite rebellion of 1715, described a brave march of rebels

through several villages; but a "fox unluckily crossing the road, drew off a considerable detachment, who clapped spurs to their horses, and pursued him with whoops and halloos, till we had lost sight of them ..." (*Works*, ed. G. W. Greene, 3.15).

[15] David Lodge, *Language of Fiction* (London, 1966), p. 76.

[16] "The Voices of Henry Fielding: Style in *Tom Jones*," in *The Augustan Milieu: Essays Presented to Louis A. Landa*, ed. Miller, Rothstein, and Rousseau (Oxford, 1970), pp. 262-88.

[17] *As You Like It*, 3.3.49-50.

[18] "Postscript" to the *Odyssey*; ed. Maynard Mack, et al., *The Twickenham Pope*, 10.382-86.

[19] *Ibid.*, p. 386.

[20] Fielding's preface to the second edition of Sarah Fielding's *David Simple* offers evidence of how naturally he tended to think of the prose-epic (i.e., romance) in terms of the *Odyssey*.

[21] Pope, p. 389.

Made in the USA
Monee, IL
15 February 2022